D1260131

COUNTER-CLOCK-WISE

Books by Michael Drury

How to Get Along with People
Advice to a Young Wife from
an Old Mistress
The Inward Sea
The Everyday Miracles
This Much and More
Every Whit Whole: The Adventure
of Spiritual Healing

COUNTER-CLOCK-WISE

Reflections of a Maverick

Michael Drury

author of

Advice to a Young Wife from an Old Mistress

Counterclockwise: Reflections of a Maverick
Michael Drury

First published in the United States of America in 1987 by the Walker Publishing Company, Inc.

Published simultaneously in Canada by John Wiley & Sons Canada, Limited, Rexdale, Ontario.

Library of Congress Cataloging-in-Publication Data
Drury, Michael.
Counterclockwise: Reflections of a Maverick.
1. Aging—Miscellanea. I. Title.
HQ1061.D78 1987 305.2′6 86-24680
ISBN 0-8027-0942-7

Printed in the United States of America

10 9 8 7 6 5 4 3 2 1

CONTENTS

I

WHAT IS OLD ANYWAY?

Come in, let me take your coat. Blowy out there, h'm? Here, let me look at you. I never thought we'd meet. Who is this college student wanting to interview me about getting old? I wrote three answers to your letter, saying no, impossible, too naked—but something always stopped me from mailing them. I pretended not to know what it was, but I knew. All my working life, interviewing others has been part of my job, and I know only too well how much gets revealed that one never intends. Cats out of bags all over the place. But where would my career be if many people hadn't allowed me into their private worlds? Graciously or reluctantly, they did it. You were my chance to repay a long debt, and—here we are. You look fine. I expect I can stand it if you can.

Come through to the kitchen if you don't mind;

we can start talking while I get lunch on the table. Oh, no trouble. It's only an omelet with garden vegetables, and apple tart with real cream from a real cow. A man I know runs a small dairy herd. Jerseys. They're gorgeous. Would you care for coffee now?

Well, I like to cook. I've done it for a living twice—it makes a change from sitting at the typewriter—and to me there's something halfway holy about kitchens. The whole staggering human enterprise started right here. Cooking fires were the first gathering places, where mankind began to collect into families and to worship. Our word *focus* is Latin for fireplace, hearth, altar. It's the kitchen that tells about a house, always. Persian rugs and brocade sofas mean nothing if the kitchen's dreary or ill-equipped or laid out like a golf course.

In a sense you could say age is like a kitchen. It's the focal point of a life, even if it does come last, the place where it all comes together—or doesn't. That last part—that it might not add up to anything—may be what scares people; I'm not sure. Me, I like it hugely. The last half of life is more complex than the first, if only because one has more pieces to juggle, but it also outclasses the first half hands down. If that isn't so, why do we lament so bitterly when someone dies young? You'd expect us to be glad. Look here: if age is no good, then life itself is no good; it's as simple as that. We're hoodwinking ourselves and lying to the young. But I don't believe it.

I find these years immensely sophisticated, for one thing. Means I know better what I'm doing. That's not to say I've got it all mastered—that would be dull. But when one has hung around long enough to have been lost and found several times over, to have been somebody and nobody, loved and hated, sick and recovered, you learn what integrity is. It's going with the forces, not against, and yet holding your own in the midst—and this borders on divinity. Sorry to sound religious, but the genius of humanity is being more than the sum of its parts, and that extra something is what one's beginning to possess in old age. Or maybe it is possessing us.

Do you know John Muir's essay on a windstorm in the forest? He climbed a Douglas fir in the Sierra Nevada and let himself get whiplashed in a gale. Some time around 1875. It was a blamed fool thing to do; he could have been struck by lightning or pitched to the ground a hundred feet below. But he came out of it drunk on the ferocious splendor of nature and his own daring. He wanted the entire populace up in trees for the next blow. I recommend getting old along the same lines. Not lashing down everything loose and stuffing cotton in one's ears, but going up high somewhere and riding it out. You'll get slammed around a little, but what of it? Absolute security is absolute stasis, and after sixty what is one hoarding life for anyway?

Age is hard—I'm not saying it isn't—and even dangerous, but that's not the same thing as ignominy. It's only the weight of circumstantial evidence that makes us think otherwise. I was slow to grasp that, but I don't suppose I'm more than usually backward. Two critical events in midlife brought me to a standstill and clued me in. One was the breakup of an eighteen-year marriage; the other, somewhat later, was the loss of longstanding markets for my writing.

A week after the divorce my lawyer came to take me to lunch. He stood looking out the window of my new and—since I had almost no furniture—barren apartment and said softly, "I could almost envy you. You wake up every morning to possibility, and that doesn't happen to most people after twenty." I caught my breath. I happened to know he was most delightfully married and wasn't extolling divorce. Nor was it exactly news that all endings involve new beginnings, but here was something more: the perception that endings are not failure but in their way are an achievement. Without them there could be no newness at any time. To start over without furniture—without the habiliments I had accumulated—was to have restored to me some properties of youth: the open-endedness, the sense of adventure. When one has been very tired, such knowledge is a cup of cool spring water.

The dissolution of markets for my work came gradually through the impact of television on public reading habits, the economic muddle of inflation, the social-sexual revolution of the 1960s that left me on the beach, too skeptical to rock and roll with the waves. Then I noticed a fourth factor.

An editor I had worked for and respected many years criticized an article I published elsewhere for being a tone poem. He meant it wasn't journalistic enough—no statistics, no citing of experts, no hard analysis. I wasn't angry—he was quite right—but I was enlightened. The piece was widely praised and I knew it to be the best I'd done so far, and suddenly I understood that the markets had not left me behind, I had left them. It was time to move on. Took me several years to assimilate that; it meant regaining my amateur standing, and that was more drastic than I expected, financially and professionally. But I did it, and it scares me now only to think I might have missed the turning. Or refused it—that's the real danger and it is our own danger, the temptation to slam the door on possibility when it masquerades as failure.

Hear me if you can in this if in nothing else: a satisfactory life has to be *crafted,* and never more so than in old age when one has acquired the tools and the skills. First one must see age for what it is—not disaster but a different mode—and then decide what one wants from it, or in it. If you don't want *something,* you sure as hellfire aren't going to get anything, unless maybe by dumb luck and that doesn't advance one much. Age is the culmination of all one has believed and dared and experienced up till then. If you have been wrong about much—and which of us has not?—take a bow. If you can see that, you are no longer fooled by it and are free to build on better knowledge. Proves your life hasn't been wasted, and that's no petty accomplishment.

No, it's not too late. Time still comes in the same size—twenty-four-hour lots, though in youth we imagine the lots are interminable. How much time is enough? One moment, the blink of an eye, is enough to be swept away by an idea. Up to a point, I admire those who salvage what they can and go bravely on—it's better than moping—but they are still in the wrong ballpark. The amount of time left is precisely not the issue. To be old is to have evolved into a new dimension where time-based, object-encrusted measurements no longer have any bearing. It is something like what religion calls "turning" or conversion, and what psychology means by gaining a new mind-set—the acquired group of ideas, habits, and skills whereby we locate ourselves in the general scheme of things—*Set* in this sense meaning not only a cluster of mental images but also jelled, settled-ness, a reliability within which we move accurately without having to take thought in advance for every action.

Until, that is, a changed environment requires a new arrangement, a different kind of knowledge. Like astronauts coping with zero gravity when feet *ought* to stay down and heads up, but don't. Or trying to make a foreign language into real talk while one is still translating every word. Or getting lost in the Pentagon, which happened to me once. That building has five nasty sides to it, laid out in concentric rings, and no amount of four-sided logic will ever get one found again. The management also plays tricks like reversing all the Up escalators to Down at quitting time. I had to be rescued by an assistant secretary's secretary when I failed to arrive at the appointed hour.

And there is the same alarmed bewilderment on the dark morning when one wakes up old, no pretending any more. Here too, the rules have been switched without warning and one wants to beat against the walls and howl. But that's only because you're trying to cram the new situation into a mind-set that has been transcended.

You know anything about flying a plane? Neither do I except what a pilot friend tells me. He says the hardest part is getting rid of your earth-based common sense. A plane is not just a car with wings, nor is the sky a road, and in the air common sense often goes backwards. Suppose one is dropping down to a landing and sees ahead a line of trees he is not going to clear. Every instinct he's got yells at him to get that nose up fast, which is the worst possible move; the plane will only sink lower. What he should do is stick the nose *down,* which will increase the speed and that in turn increases lift, and the plane will hedgehop neatly over the trees. But it's not enough merely to know that; it takes a mind-and-body feel. Otherwise, in the crunch one will act on the ingrained conviction that it's mad to aim at an object that can kill you if you hit it. Would-be pilots wash out when they cannot let go of what always worked before. People wash out on aging for the same reason.

Living old is not merely an extended adulthood, any more than adulthood is elongated youth. One is transposed into a different medium that demands an altered awareness of interconnections. If the new mental image is correct, you will do well almost spontaneously. If one persists adamantly in the dear familiar habits of thinking and doing, a debacle is inevitable.

The demand upon us all is to put away childish things, but one rather assumes it's mostly finished by eighteen or so. It comes as a shock to find it's just as imperative at eighty. There are things suitable and things unsuitable all along the line. The enthusiasm that sparkles in the young is embarrassing and half-baked in a grown-up. The middle-aged devotion to rank, properties, office, committees, influence, and greetings in the marketplace is appropriate and even admirable, but it ought to be tempered later. If at eighty one has not emerged into deeper perceptions and stiller joys, it is to invite pity.

Old people have not ceased to care or believe, but they use emotion to different ends. Because they have not got to impress, not even themselves, their own emotions no longer dazzle them. One does outgrow the gee-whiz, look-what-happened-to-me stage of consciousness, and that's emancipation. One realizes that there truly is nothing new under the sun, and it doesn't matter who gets credit for what. In ancient Rome emancipation was a legal status signifying complete release from paternal power; henceforth, one answered for oneself before the law, for good or ill. Perhaps the most exciting facet of aging—and what I meant when I said it was sophisticated—is that heady sense of emancipation, of having arrived at full identity.

Oh, that makes me edgy, that cliché about age being akin to childhood. Yes, there is simplification, but you must not confuse it with the simpleness of children. A child is simple out of ignorance: it knows no other way to be, and in its season that has great charm. Mature simplicity is conceptual. It selects and knows, and selects *because* it knows; it is distilled from long and hard experience, pared down, discriminative.

What the old and children may have in common is the facing of untried territory. The one comes out of mystery into birth and faces an alien world; the other, at home in the world, is preparing to return to the earlier half-forgotten mystery, and the prospect before each fills them with mingled eagerness and alarm. Children, unless they have been badly warped, soon opt for eagerness. Sheer animal spirits if nothing else draw them into life. Old people, unless they have been singularly blessed, are inclined to hang back. Somehow we have to find ways of persuading people that keeping on with the incorrigible adventure to the end is the supreme purpose of any and every human life.

I don't think Americans know *how* to be old, and they don't want to know. Age doesn't fit the rootin' shootin' live-it-up formula and that makes the establishment uneasy as cats, so it does what cats do—spits, fluffs out its hair and comes in broadside to present the biggest possible image. Gross bulk (misread as majority rule) must overbear all obstacles, including old age (misread as used up, ineffectual). The bureaucrats can't quite rub us out, so they kill us with kindness. The old are now discovered as a class to be reckoned with, as juveniles were forty years ago, and that's not all bad. In a society hooked on numbers there are times when only a collective voice can budge that society. But age is also the most acutely individual of life's hitches, and if an old citizen wants to go up in a balloon or live in a cave, a really just society would leave him to it.

I am leery of planners and managers who want to arrange me for my own good. Who made them deciders of my good? I refuse to be a case history, a specimen, a blip on a chart, a room number, exhibit A. Dotty old thing, likes her hair straight, won't get a decent perm; got a mind of her own, that one. Who else's mind should I have, for the love of heaven?

I'm not always as prickly as that sounds, but one

does grow weary of being told what one wants, what one is like; what to wear, what to eat, what to believe, what to fear, what to settle for. I am not the old, I'm *an* old; there's an ocean of difference. The scat-thinkers call me young old—means I'm pushing seventy—and they are fond of reminding me I ain't seen nothing yet; the goblins will get me, they get everybody. Maybe, but I can sooner scare myself with my own desert places, as Robert Frost called them. I don't need permission to think. If the coming years are going to require bravery from me, then I don't intend to be cheated of my occasion to be brave. It's all part of living, and how shall I learn the craft except I practice now with whatever's going for me or against me?

Oh, bother loneliness—it's sinister but not fatal, and it's a bad mistake to suppose that other people are the only remedy. That's using others to serve one's own ends, scarcely a reliable way to make oneself likable. Besides, there is no isolation so deadly as company without companionship, being with those for whom one feels no congeniality and with whom one cannot even communicate. Look at the long-married couples who sit at dinner night after night and do not speak.

What one is lonely *for* is the question, and it is not necessarily people. It can be events, places, action, one's own mind. That, I think, is always a factor and is the reason the mere presence of others cannot fill up the gap. Nor is loneliness as dire as its reputation. It can bring privacy, unity, self-knowledge—if one turns it in those directions and doesn't grab at any distraction to avoid noticing that one is alone.

It has been said that woman's long search for her place in the sun has a basis in the fact that Eve, unlike Adam, never had a chance to be alone in the world. The language is mythical but the point is cogent. And there is a folk-saying that girl babies are born a whole year older than boys, an allusion to advanced female maturity that annoys and perplexes men as much as male precedence grieves women. There may well be a correlation between these three things: age, solitude, and self-determination. St. Thomas Aquinas suggested that to be a person at all is willingness to be alone, for the word stems from the Latin *per se una*, one by itself, though I don't think etymologists are agreed. I do know that somewhere in every life there comes a time to be good company for oneself, and this self-possession is strangely attractive, drawing to itself as by an inverse law the friends whose absence seemed so desolating at the outset.

Old people as a class are specially fitted to do one thing nobody else can do—or is doing anyway. By reason of distance they are able to consider the long run, pay attention to outcomes, ask sticky questions; and by reason of detachment they can discern wholes rather than fragments. That's what wisdom is, I think. The old have no axe to grind; they won't be around to lap up short-term perks, and this gives them a rare leverage. They are not entangled by expedience.

The world is beyond question immersed in a pea soup of science and its offspring, technology; and it is the acknowledged purpose of science not to accept things as they are but to take them apart, to probe, to discover what lies beneath the surface and, where desired, to rearrange it. Never mind who desires, that's another matter. Coming as it did to a world steeped in superstition and often helpless in the face of things as they were, science seemed like the great answer to man's destiny. It was, and is, so effective that it has by now acquired some of the faults it set out to remedy—absolutism, infallibility, elitism, even idolatry. It has become so pervasive and complex that it takes apart even itself, isolating each scientist in his own miniscule patch of a single limited field, utterly unconcerned with what lies outside it. A duly awed and sometimes grateful public hastens to copy the trappings at every turn.

The man who comes to fix my washer will not touch the faucet to which it is attached, if that's where the trouble lies; I must call a different repairman. Teachers present their subjects with no concern for their relation to education as a whole; they have not heard that education is any sort of whole. Even the department store clerk who sells coats has no idea where socks are located and is offended by the inquiry. The patient who died although the operation was a success was a routine vaudeville joke when I was a child, but today transplant surgeons go before TV cameras to announce that very thing, and nobody finds it absurd.

We are dominated by parts-science and parts-scientists, fiercely competitive with one another and proud of their ignorance outside their own circumscribed specialities—after all, that's what qualifies them as experts. They largely can't or won't communicate even with other scientists, let alone the lay public, because argot is another marker setting them off as special. If you ask me—and nobody has or will—

that's what afflicted the space shuttle that blew up. There was no conspiracy and no intentional negligence; it was just a bunch of specialists not talking to one another and unable to see the forest for the trees. It goes on all the time.

Old people have the skills to step into the breach and maybe even to save civilization from chopping itself to bits. They have the necessary noninvolvement to ask questions about values, ends, wholes. Not all of them may want the ability, but they've got it just by being old if they care to use it. A certain metropolitan police chief has said that age is the one practical means of rehabilitating criminals. At twenty-three, he said, a man can see today, tomorrow, and just possibly the day after. If he wants something, he takes it by violence and sees nothing wrong with that because for him it is now or never. The same man at forty-three perceives the transience of crime and will work toward what he wants because he can think beyond immediacy. I would add that at sixty-three the man sees how to want better things, and that's the next step in his personal evolution. It takes age to understand much about the situation we are in; that too is more or less what wisdom is.

It puzzles me why erosion of the cuticle constitutes all the literature on age, with economics running a remote second. All other kinds of aging are ignored. Well, take minds and souls; they get old too. So do tastes and loves, ambitions and beliefs. Love isn't very reliable until it has aged. Fear when it gets old tends to disappear and even strangely becomes an ally. When you have been looking down a gun barrel long enough to get bored and say, "Oh, go ahead and shoot," fear sighs and backs away—and then you see all along that it was of your own making. Faults and weaknesses turn into strengths when at last one learns that it was never required to possess all talents—people could not stand us if we were paragons—and then you are able not only to stand but to remit the faults of others. Beliefs grow pliable with years. One doesn't necessarily abandon them, but they flow around one as gracefully as a toga or a graduation gown.

Sometimes people say, "I never chose to be old," as though to exonerate themselves from blame. But then what? Did somebody else choose and thrust them into age like Aztecs being tossed into the volcano? Well, no, but circumstances brought them to this unhappy pass. People who think that thought it all their lives, and age is just one more occasion to cry foul and throw in the sponge. I want to shake them. If you can't face reality at sixty-five, when will you ever? The American philosopher William Ernest Hocking said the same circumstances occur to good men and bad, but *free* men take control. To put off taking charge is to fail at one's own humanity. I am not trying to dis-invent science—I'm not that stupid. But I agree with Hocking that human beings are a great deal more than the mere instruments of science or of nature. The dismissal of that something more as inconsequential is what plagues our crestfallen era and makes aging within it so terrifying for many.

I may not have deliberately chosen to be old because I too was once young and unknowing, but I promise you I choose it now, every day, with my eyes open and utter gladness of heart. Consider the alternative: Without aging I should have remained young and unknowing. Would any of us, I wonder, really be smart enough of our own volition to stand still and hear and observe and frame a dialogue with the universe unless age compelled us to do it?

Age is not a penalty, it's the homestretch, and there is natural pride and a modest glory in having got here. You can see that even in a very old animal—a dignity, an aloofness. Reaching the homestretch is evidence of having stayed the distance, even if not of having run a good race. It's better to come in 14th or 195th than to have opted out along the course.

Maybe I am a bit offbeat. In earlier years I liked to say when I got old I would become a character, wear green tennis shoes and carry a string bag and say impossible things. My friends would wail, "What do you think you are now!" I do believe we age very much as we have lived—that is to say, in character. And so I ask myself a thousand times how much of what I'm saying arises from my particular situation—an unconventional career; a taste for being much alone; the pleasure I find in books; the liberty that is conferred by being on amiable terms with the Creator. I try to be severe in estimating this, because it's too easy to extrapolate from one's own necessarily limited experience.

But I don't think I am deceiving myself. For one thing, I asked other people in widely differing fields and they largely concurred with my approach to age. For another thing, I don't subscribe to the view that writers and artists are a special breed. I often tell beginning writers that their job is not to be wonderful but to set forth some portion of our common human adventure, and the better they do it, the more they deserve to call themselves writer. And third, gumption is the property of no particular class, no race or occupation or level of schooling, no sex or age. Important? It's critical. No gumption, no gusto—of that much I am sure, however old one is or isn't.

II

A REASONABLE BODY

We had better clear the decks of bodies before anything else. Declining health is not my idea of a darling topic, but it is, alas, presumed to be the very essence of aging, and if I don't make plain why I disagree, you can scuttle everything else I say on the ground that people are not able to make the effort. One cannot prevent age and there is no reason to try. To be old is the unifying portion of the cycle, as natural as a flower dropping its petals. I sometimes make potpourri, and I have found that when I gather the petals too soon—too young—they tend to rot rather than dry and they smell funny. But if I time the picking just as the flowers begin to shed, they retain both aroma and some color.

Of course the body deteriorates. Life as we know it is a slow dying from day one but that's not necessarily illness. Moses was said to be 120 years old when he died, and "his eye was not dim nor his natural force abated." He was eighty when he undertook his vocation of leading the Israelites out of captivity. Put up a fierce battle against the idea, too—who wouldn't at that age?—but he got the job done and made a difference to all history. It is recorded that he got dreadfully tired at times, so tired that he couldn't raise his arms above his head, a gesture that was needed as a signal, and two strong men were appointed to stand on either side and prop them up. Moses wasn't so different from us. The body wilts and energy flags, but those are not the only facts nor even the most important.

Do you ever go swimming absolutely naked? It is a queer sensation, a little foolish and a lot exotic. I know people who hate it because it makes them feel defenseless and displaced. It's a fine thing for old people to do though, if they can find a spot lonely enough. One is only half one's gravity weight in water, and it gives practice in managing an altered body-sense. The unfamiliarity does make one feel evicted from one's own skin, but after a bit something silly and lovely takes over, sleek, lithe, almost body-less. If one can take even a fraction of that loss-and-gain back to dry land, it can make a difference to the later years, both in sickness and in health.

What first dismays us about aging is vanity, the loss of what we hoped and believed was attractiveness. All young creatures are more or less beautiful because they still have the dew on them, but it is a beauty more shallow than we like to admit or the waning wouldn't shatter us. I have seen old faces, on both women and men, that made me gasp with pleasure and offer an inward prayer: Let me look like that when my time comes. Oh, Casey Stengel, for one, the famed baseball manager. Have you never seen an old person stop conversations and turn heads just by walking into a room? Stengel was like that. It takes more than perfect features and a springtime glance; it takes experience, self-knowledge, an air of meeting life as its peer, a mix of caring and detachment. Nobody is born with that ready-made; it's earned by years of daring. Nor is it a feminine prerogative; it belongs equally to either sex, though it's not sexless, either.

The French Nobel writer Albert Camus once said that after forty every man is responsible for his own face. It's a sobering thought. The first time I saw Robert Frost he came to my university to speak, and he was sixty-five then. Twenty years later I wrote a long magazine article about him when he was nearing eighty-six. I had never seen anything but the white-haired patriarch, but now among the early papers I came across several pictures of him as a young man. In one library there hung a life-size, three-quarter-length photograph made at thirty-six, and he was strikingly handsome. He *looked* like a poet, not somebody's grandfather; I knew beyond doubt that women had found him devastating, a thing that hadn't even occurred to me before; there was a definite arrogance. That photo troubled me; here was a man within the man I thought I knew, and I wondered if I did.

Then on the last day I stood with him in the kitchen of his Vermont cabin—another kitchen—trying to say good-bye in such a way as to include thank-you and much else. It's a curious business, writing biography. One lives a little time—warily—two lives at once. Suddenly I knew with force that this was the real person, not the beautiful young man in the photograph. This was the face he was responsible for, real as only full age can be real, because it is, by that much, more finished.

One does not, as Frost would have put it, attain to such authenticity until, among other things, the body stops getting in the way, which for most of us means after it has begun to decline so that one can cease admiring it. As the underlying bone shapes the contours, so the armature of the spirit hones development of them, and a face that has had a long run can surpass any degree of early glamour. Face-lifting cannot work that transformation; artifice only delays the reckoning that results in the real thing.

By no means do I damn all plastic surgery. I went to college with a man who is now one of this country's top plastic surgeons, and I have a stunned regard for what he does for battle-scarred soldiers and the victims of accident or fire or malformation. But he will not perform cosmetic surgery without careful interviews to ascertain why the patient wants it and what he expects to happen afterward. You might be surprised to know how often it is literally "he." Men too agonize over the loss of their good looks and in some ways are less equipped than women to handle it. It comes on them later and more abruptly. Women learn at an early date to accommodate a body not always at its glowing best or submissive to their wishes.

What attracts us to one another is not so much vitality as validity—strong presence, fertility of ideas, resourcefulness in the teeth of life's recalcitrance; wit, fair-mindedness, autonomy. Look here: would you like to be the age you are now and have the body of an infant? Can you imagine the monstrous creature lying on a six-foot bed in a diaper, with curved limbs and a head too big for the rest of it, playing with its toes and blowing bubbles? Then you can understand why I do not yearn for the body of a nubile young woman, or any other age that would belie my years of living and learning. Vanity is a form of dishonesty and I am well pleased to have got beyond that stage. Oh yes, I protested a bit at first—not much, I was never a beauty—but it was a poor sort of response and I knew it.

Make the most of whatever the Lord gave—or your ancestral genes if you like—I'm all for that. But make it at every level. I'd rather look like an interested old woman than an ersatz young one. If one's entire strategy is combat against an implacable enemy, then that's what the face will reflect—fighting, not living—and laid-on camouflage will never persuade others one is winning the war.

Well, the matter of physical health is trickier. More is at stake and more outsiders are bent on getting into the act with sterner claims. Every so often some doctor makes news by announcing that age in itself is not a disease, but nobody takes much notice, least of all his colleagues. Think of all the lovely money to be lost if they did. If age is not chronic illness, you would never know it from society. Government, big business, advertising, technology, certainly medicine and even journalism harangue daily on the hazards to old people in staying alive. One cannot listen to the weather report without being cautioned that the heat wave or the cold wave or the humidity or the high winds are excessively dangerous to the old. Breathing in those atmospheres is difficult and one should watch it, whatever that means.

Everyone over fifty-five is more or less compelled to have a second career body-watching—and not the kind done on beaches. Yet any competent clock-maker will tell you not to be nervously winding or resetting your watch all day; it only ruins the mechanism's fine-tuning. How well do you function if at every turn you must examine your efforts for failure? It's crazy. Age may not officially be sick, but it is deemed to be "at risk"; the old are prodded into constant self-scrutiny between visits to the body shop and congratulated if they discover some malady. Good boy, see how clever you are. Any society that makes a virtue of anxiety sooner or later reflects its own sickness back upon its people. The coercion is staggering. It is the old citizen's equivalent of teenage peer pressure. One would have to be a stone statue not to be influenced by it, if only to resist.

Oh, mercy, the odds on liability to some killer-disease—a pitch word if ever there was one—mean nothing for me or for any other one person. Odds are pure abstraction, even at the race track or gaming tables. To become *my* odds, even by their own criteria, they'd have to allow for my genetic heritage—how far back, I wonder, and why do only sick forebears count; have the healthy ones no genes to contribute?—my daily patterns of eating, sleeping, exercise, and all that; whether I drink or smoke and how much; the work I do or don't; my medical history, if any; and endless other data *ad nauseum*. Just so. I could still defy their odds, like Winston Churchill living into his nineties doing all the wrong things; despite the brandy and cigars and excess weight, the lifelong bouts of melancholy, the disinclination to exercise. The pundits pronounce Churchill an exception, but hang it, *I'm* an exception and so's everybody else taken one at a time, which is the only possible way life is lived in case they haven't noticed, and the odds are meaningless and I rest my case.

Health care is a misnomer—and another pitch word. It's *ill* health that everyone's on about, but it's bad for the company image to say so. Doctors cannot tell one what health is, nor even offer a norm or baseline upon which one's own health is calculated. It's all a matter of being better than you were yesterday or worse than last year—like an endless war where peace is no longer the goal because nobody remembers what that is or if it ever was. The day-to-day warfare is measured in statistics—casualties, body count, air raids, number of bombs, towns and bases demolished—until tabulation becomes the measure of life itself. Fighting nations often do not know what the people do when they are not fighting, and take pride in the not knowing. Industrial nations have forgotten what health is and cannot imagine what people do when they are not battling sickness.

Health is a personal statement, an immeasurable private experience, which means it is not scientific and thus readily dismissed by the science of curing disease. A first principle in scientific method is the elimination of variables, and human beings are outrageously variable, thus they cannot be allowed to figure in scientific procedure. Even when they feel on top of the world, they are not absolved from harboring some fiendish disease that only high-tech probing can ferret out and zap into oblivion. To me that smacks of medieval demons in twentieth-century clothing.

A Swiss cancer specialist, much frowned upon by his peers, was quoted to me as having said that if you could cut up a perfectly healthy body without killing it, you'd find as many as a hundred small tumors that build up and dissolve spontaneously, and nobody knows why. He believed they might be part of the natural immune process, and that medicine was too hasty about rooting them out. He would like to see a little more respect for the body's powers.

That man has long since died, and I never thoroughly checked out his statement about tumors, but his use of the word *respect* caught my ear. When I realized that if I wanted definitions of health I'd have to make my own, one of my first attempts was this: Health is being approached in all circumstances with respect for my human nature, and vice versa—approaching others the same way. You may say that's nothing to do with health, but it is. Health is a good deal more than the absence of some illness, and any patient who knows that can outthink any doctor who doesn't.

One day a doctor addressed me as "young lady," which is rude and condescending, but I let it go because I was so amazed by what followed. I had refused a certain procedure, and he said sternly, "Young lady, I'm in charge here." I was surprised into retorting, "What on earth makes you think so?" It was his turn to be surprised, and I added, "I pay you, you don't pay me, and it's been my experience that he who pays calls the shots." After a moment he said, "But you pay me for my professional judgment." I agreed and said I would weigh it carefully, but it was my body, my life, and in the long run the decisions were mine. He replied, "If you persist in that attitude, I have no choice but to dismiss you from my care." That, I told him, I could respect. I wrote out a check, went home, and promptly recovered from my ailment. Not perhaps the most propitious way to do it but it taught me something, and I now insist upon a preliminary interview with any physician—as I had always done with other professionals, lawyers, accountants, agents—to see if there is mutual respect before we attempt to work together.

That's not always easy when the professional is apt to be younger than oneself. One can feel the derision caroming off the walls, but if you make up your mind going in that you are entitled to open-mindedness, and if he cannot bear that, you are being more professional than he is, you'll come off unruffled, even amused, and wiser. It's better to know where one stands in advance of a crisis. I've had doctors flatly refuse to see me at all for a mere discussion, and that's fine. It tells me what I need to know without costing a cent.

Medical monism is endemic throughout the field and rampant toward the old because they themselves are guilty and apologetic about being old. They figure they are on the slope no matter what they say or do. I think many are easily cowed because they're bored, and starved for drama, even melodrama. One of the characters in Lawrence Durrell's *Alexandria Quartet* says that all sickness is an acute form of self-importance. I don't know that I go along with *all,* and importance is all right if it's confined to the literal level of import, of meaning. Meaning is one of life's major purposes. But Durrell's remark startles one awake.

Ill health generates a lot of attention, some of it highly trained, and if attention has been lacking of late, being sick is not without attractions. It furnishes a focus; one is in demand for appointments, the phone rings, mail increases. Doctors are "important" and expensive; it's easy to conclude, like any sycophant, that being in their cohort enhances one's own notability. Surely the limelight spills over a little? I have no quarrel with that if it's what one really wants, but it speaks poorly of a society with so little regard for anyone over sixty that many are diddled into makeshift reasons to be living.

Health is partly boldness, being responsible for one's own events and conditions, come what may. On those terms some people are scared of health; it sounds suspiciously like being winkled out of familiar grooves, like having to grow up. We are a nation besotted with the quick fix. But is that health? Is it living? One cannot abdicate from half of life, the dark side, without also shunning the bright. On an overcast day the light is flat, dull, uninteresting. Only sunlight brings out shadows, and only shadows give depth, distinctness, form. I wouldn't give two pins for a life without darkness. Health is an expression of full-scale humanity; the belief that one can be attained at the sacrifice of the other is oxymoronic.

I'm *not* peddling hair shirts, I'm arguing for living one's oldness as opposed to getting rid of it, which is manifestly unworkable and breeds defeat. I'm pleading for intelligence as a means of coping with age in all its ramifications. For examining loss of vigor to see what it has to teach us. For handling pain and sickness in such a manner as to reach new and sophisticated levels of selfhood. For recognizing the whole lifespan as evolution of the personality.

I'm not convinced we come apart piecemeal as modern medicine presumes, nor, therefore, that a system that seeks to repair us bit by bit can be effectual. A freethinking English doctor and psychiatrist named E. Graham Howe—a thorn in the side of the Royal Society all his life—said that healing depends upon acceptance of the rejected part of ourselves. There is something recognizable to me in that, and it's why I say it's dangerous to reject aging—it invites the very thing one is trying to evade. Another thinker, Ivan Illich, an international writer who mows down sacred cows, says in his book *Medical Nemesis* that children and savages have to be taught to localize pain. When they hurt, they hurt all over, not just in their stomach or head or arm. That too, I have myself experienced, and more recently than in childhood. For all their expertise, up-to-date methods of treatment may not be as advanced as we suppose.

You are probably too young to remember a poem by Oliver Wendell Holmes known as "The Wonderful One-Hoss Shay," though that isn't its proper title. Holmes called it "The Deacon's Masterpiece." Shay is a corruption of *chaise* which Americans mistook for plural. It was a two-wheeled buggy favored long ago by rural preachers and doctors, light and fast but given like modern cars to frequent breakdowns. Holmes's deacon got fed up and had his own shay built of the finest materials and crafted so that it could take the stress equally at all points. A century passed and the buggy had outlasted several owners and looked fine except for "a general flavor of mild decay." Then one day it fell apart on the road in a heap of rubble, "all at once," Holmes wrote, "and nothing first,/just as bubbles do when they burst."

That poem was taught to schoolchildren in my day as a lesson in diligence and good workmanship, and we thought it quaint and pious even then. In high school, though, our third-year English teacher pointed out that Holmes was a medical doctor and that he called the shay a masterpiece. What light did that shed? It took us a while and much prodding, but we finally realized that the shay might be a human body, a thing magnificently framed to bear the stresses of a lifetime, and Dr. Holmes could be implying that we too are designed to live and die all of a piece. That didn't make the poem into great literature, but wisdom is not to be skimped, wherever found. In some areas of Japan, Russia, and South America, and among certain Indian tribes, old people do die in that fashion. They don't sicken, they just come to a stop.

A curious aspect of health is that when one has

got it, one is not conscious of it in detail. I don't know I have a stomach unless it is ailing. I am not aware that my hand performs a miracle in peeling an orange unless for some reason it cannot do it. Even sexual desire, which most people welcome and take pride in, makes itself known by discomfort, what an old show tune dubbed "that pleasant ache," and stays that way until it is relieved or subsides by itself, much like a headache. Health is a quiet asset. That's not to say one has to carry on like a dockhand; it's common sense to pace oneself. But if you cannot swim a few laps or play tennis or walk a brisk mile, whatever your fancy, without blowing like a whale; if you cannot weed the garden or stay up two extra hours reading or watching a ballgame without dragging through the next day—in heaven's name don't settle for that just because you're not young.

More than twenty years ago a friend of mine was appearing in a Broadway musical in which she did a short but vigorous dance with a lad less than half her age—and size. She was a big woman, tall, heavy boned, and weighed around 180 pounds. The pair of them were so incongruous and their footwork so clever that the routine stopped the show every night and there were always encores. It made me breathless just to watch them, and I asked my friend how she could do it night after night without collapsing, and she replied, "By doing it night after night. You can do anything you are accustomed to."

I decided right then that though I could not stop getting old, I could at least maintain a pliable body, and I asked one of the show's dancers to devise an exercise program for me that I might carry into the future. He did it and I still work with it. He told me two things I find constantly useful. The first was, "If you work up a sweat, you're doing it wrong. You're not training for the Olympics. At your age what you want is flexibility and long lines, so we'll go for stretching, bending, breathing." I was somewhat insulted at being told I didn't know how to breathe, but let me tell you a thing: breathing is a talent most people don't know they've got. It actually tastes good, and you can use it to cure minor ailments like headache or sleeplessness.

The dancer's other advice was to forget doing it by the clock. "You're not doing time in the clink," he said. "You're learning to feel delicious, and if you make that your gauge, you'll know when it's enough. Seven minutes that you enjoy are better than half an hour of drudgery that you find reasons to skip." I sometimes wonder where that man is now and whether he'd be pleased to know one old woman can sit on the floor, legs straight out on either side, and lay her chin on the carpet—because of his sane teaching.

I suppose I'm proud of it, but there's more to it than being a phenomenon. It affects the way I move, which in turn affects the way I face the world and the way it faces me, that is to say how I see challenges and setbacks—as primary or secondary, as problems or merely living. Health is a lot like money in that a modicum of both is needed for survival, and that both are insatiable. If one becomes obsessed with health or money, or waits around for a sufficiency of either before beginning to live, one comes up to the finish line and discovers one has missed living altogether. Survival isn't a lifework, by itself it cannot satisfy. Health, like housework, has to be attended to, but it's background. One ought to do it up as ably as one can and get on with life.

III

THE REPOSSESSION OF TIME

One of the queer effects of aging is banging one's nose on infinity. Meaning that one discovers he never knew the first thing about time—you will, I trust, grant me an occasional use of "he" and "his"? I was brought up to the grammatical rule that in the absence of particulars the male pronoun loses its sexuality, and I do not find that this stigmatizes my own.

To return to time: all these years one has been living through it, steeped in it, soaked by it—not as old friends perhaps, but then as old enemies, which is by far the more intimate link. An enemy always surprises, always demands more than you can perform—had any intention of performing—so that in measuring up, you exceed the old limits and think, "This way to myself!" There is no greater bond.

I heard an RAF pilot say much the same thing

about the German fliers he was trying to shoot out of the English sky in 1940. It was kill or be killed, and he was constantly outnumbered, yet he felt a fierce respect for them and theirs for him. At times they exchanged a grin or gave a thumbs-up for a bit of good flying. They shared a comradery no earthling, military or civilian, could have fathomed. It was a deadly game they played, but by playing it well, each drove the other to new heights, not only of skill but of emotion and understanding.

An old man or woman's waltz with time is much like that. Time the implacable foe is also time the liberator; it compels one beyond where he has been in the past. Like any discipline, time's purpose is to turn one loose in the long run. Sure it's true. Look at the discipline of athletes; musicians; the mystics. All right, I shan't get philosophical, but I shall come back to athletes, the Dallas Cowboys and some others. They hold impertinent attitudes toward time; it's not a thing reserved for scholars and heavy thinkers. Right now what I'm saying is that being nudged beyond time is one half-shocking freedom that comes with age. You can't exactly plan for it, but you can let it happen.

The Zen Buddhists have some such tenet, I believe. Took me a while to get through my head how it could be done and what good it would do anyway, but now that I've got some decades behind me, I'm less stubborn. In Zen one does quite a few things—archery for one—without being told how, and after you quiet down and stop yammering for explanations, you begin to do it better. Pretty soon the thing itself begins to teach you all you want to know, inner things no amount of theory and outlining could contain. Perverse as that seems to western minds, there is no other way to master intuition consciously. So it is with time and age, which is time in a particular form. One has to be old for about ten years before it begins to reveal its secrets. Time isn't entirely hostile. It has assets, but not on the surface. One has to seek them like the game of Hide the Thimble. You are too young to have played that—an old game devised by grandmothers for rainy afternoons. They called out "Warm" or "Cold" as one got nearer or farther from the hiding place. I told a man the other day I was obsolete as a buttonhook, and he said, "What's a buttonhook?" Proved my point—fast.

St. Augustine said he knew perfectly well what he meant by time but if asked to define it, he could not. That's the way most of us feel. Everybody assumes he knows what time is and assumes, correctly, that everyone else makes the same assumption. It works, too. Stores and offices, banks and factories open at the stated hour, workers show up. Public transport runs on schedule—oh, well, with a margin for error. Universities conduct classes on a plan of hours, days, weeks. Russians, Chinese, Jews, and other cultures maintain separate religious calendars, but manage their worldly affairs according to the western calendar, which is Christian: Monday is agreed to be Monday the world over; weekends are weekends; if the summit conference begins on a Thursday, it is the same day for all parties. Civilization is fueled by time; without it the whole machinery would grind to a halt.

But in private life age comes along and blows one's

house down just as time is beginning to run out and one is clinging to the roof beams. Time, that unvarying stuff, which one has not always liked but which has glued things together for the better part of a century, is not only coming unglued itself but may not even be a stuff. How dare it?

I remember learning as a schoolgirl that it is always morning somewhere, a prosaic snippet of wisdom, but I was much taken with it. Ever a morning creature, I began at once to contrive schemes for maintaining myself at speed in an airplane so as to live in perpetual sunrise. I could see too that all days were exactly alike—Fourth of July, birthdays, the lot—and thus every morning a kind of New Year's day if you started counting with that one. Boundaries were dissolving, could dissolve, a scary thought. When one is young, scary is delicious.

There was another reason for satisfaction. My mother, who was full of late Victorian "recitations," used to quote a pious verse at me to speed my daily tasks.

If you in the morning throw minutes away,
You can't pick them up in the course of the day;
You may hurry and scurry and flurry and worry,
But you've lost them forever, forever and ay!

Loathsome piece of doggerel, but I could never offer a word in rebuttal until my fourth-grade teacher gave us that glimpse of time's made-up properties. I wasn't about to argue with my elders—in those days one didn't—but I recognized truth when I met it, as any mind does, and I hugged to myself the power it gave me.

Something not unlike that has happened now in what I am pleased to call my majority, another meltdown of time's fixity—two of them, in fact. One, time is not linear. Two, time is not quantitative. There is neither much nor little; it doesn't accumulate, cannot run out, never began. Because it would have to have begun at some *time,* so you'd need a supra-time in which to contain that event, and the question would arise whether *that* ever began, and so on forever. Forever is without end in either direction, and there you are.

Put it like this: time is not nothing, so, yes, it is real, it exists. But neither is it what we habitually call time, and in that sense, no, it is not real. You expect me to give you a neat summary of what neither St. Augustine nor anybody else can define? That's crazy. To define is, by definition, to impose limits. And I've just said time hasn't got any. Time is a foundational element in which we are suspended from birth, and we know it but do not perceive it through the senses—but that's another can of philosophical worms. It's easier to illustrate with space. We don't perceive space by sensory means either. That's evident if you go up in an airplane in the right sort of cloud cover so that you are immersed in cloud. There is no sensation of speed or direction, and if the plane turned over, you could not tell up from down.

I knew an airline pilot to whom that happened once in a hurricane at night. In those days if a plane went over 180 degrees, it knocked out all the instruments, and the crew could not be sure they'd got the aircraft right side up again. They could have been flying belly up or straight into the ground. Eventually they got low enough to see the lights of a town going by at a crazy angle and with that as a guide they were able to level the plane and land.

We perceive space only by interruptions of it—by objects *in* space that provide the necessary clues. And we accommodate time too by interruptions that we impose on it: hours, days, weeks, months, minutes, years, clocks, calendars, meridians, all the paraphernalia that give us a place to stand, like Pappus with his lever. Most of us don't want to move the earth, just our own small affairs, but pure time, like pure space, disorients us. The illuminati fine-tune it down to milliseconds and then nanoseconds. A millionth of a second, I thought, until recently a physicist told me one billionth, but that rattles me. I can find no slot for a billionth of a second. My mind wants to sneak off and hide, so I don't push it.

Anyway, whatever one's range, that's what time is to him, and he accepts the terms so axiomatically that it is hard to remember they are only terms and not the dimension itself. Some people, on first crossing the international dateline, cannot lose the uneasy feeling they've been cheated of a day or handed an extra one somehow plucked out of nowhere. That's not as silly as it might sound. We are not accustomed to time being discretionary.

When this country adopted a pay-as-you-go income tax in 1943, the entire United States Congress for all its expertise could not get into its collective dome that the basic change would be from a retroactive to a current accounting system. Whether it was *called* last year's tax or this year's, it was the same money paid into the coffers at the same time. Our neighbor Canada had done it the year before with no loss of revenue. The United States treasurer, assorted federal reserve officers, and Wall Street and corporate moneymen spent hours in committee trying to explain that it was as simple as daylight saving. But to the honorable legislators it looked suspiciously like forgiving a whole year's federal income, and that was unthinkable. What they meant was "foregoing" but "forgiving" was the word they used—which clearly shows their moralistic and emotional assessment of the subject.

In the end everyone wound up paying double taxes in that first year of the switch-over, and almost nobody protested because most people agreed with Congress. A year was a real thing and ought not to be pushed around.

I don't mock them, I've been there. Now and then I admit I'm still there. Time is so interwoven with one's world sense and his own location in it that tampering with time feels like tampering with one's identity. Quite right, too. It's me out there melting down with the edges of time, like being in a foundry, getting poured into a new mold. That's what makes this age stuff so exciting. As I have said, age has a tendency to rub one's nose in the movable nature of time, and there that enemy suddenly is, challenging you to step over the old safe boundaries, threatening to push you over, like it or not. You'd have to be deaf and dumb not to be alarmed.

Look: accept with me for the moment the idea that time is everywhere present, like space. If that is so, then it is just here, and we can move around in it at will, as we do in space—sideways, up and down, even backwards. It's more than theoretical. It's done every day without a second thought in daydreams, in sleep, in planning for the future, in memory, in recall. You'll say that's not real time but what is real time? Physicists have a reference point they call real time, but they'll tell you it's only an agreed-upon baseline enabling them to talk intelligibly with one another among a melange of times—elapsed time, mean time, atomic time, and others, including clock time, which they have to use like the rest of us to get home to dinner. Nearly anyone knows the experience of flying west for five hours and having to set his watch back three. Has the journey "really" taken only two hours or did it "really" start three hours before its departure time?

It is not time that's linear, it's us. We are one-directional creatures. That's not bad, it's not good; it just happens to be the case. What we call time is, in fact, measurements—hours, days, years, minutes, and all that which is like calling a yardstick space, and even more basically it is our sense of sequence, of events following one after the other. We take it as unarguable that night follows day. Shakespeare thought so and used it as a poetic illustration of inescapable truth. But the Babylonians and Chaldeans reckoned day from sunset, not dawn, and the Hebrew book of Genesis says, "There was evening and there was morning, one day." Again, evening and morning, a second day, and on throughout the six days of creation. Even when the figuring changed over to morning first, it was only after clocks became commonplace about 250 years ago that the new day started at midnight instead of six A.M. In religious orders the ninth hour is still three in the afternoon, and compline, the last prayer at night, is the seventh liturgical hour. Never mind, I only mention it to show that there are many kinds of time going on all around us, and real time is wherever you want to put it, provided you are consistent and that others who have to deal with you know what system you're using.

In China there are no time zones, so it is seven o'clock from Shanghai to Shofu although they are 3,000 miles apart. They must have to make allowances for the rest of the world, but time in China itself has little relation to Greenwich time. A friend in Honolulu tells me that a certain news broadcaster used to come on the air saying, "Good evening. It's ten o'clock in Hawaii, and tomorrow all over the world." I had to check that out on a global map, but it's quite genuine. Real time—ha!

Linear time is not so much wrong as provincial, and that's not to be laid to our blame. Linear time is natural and useful so long as one doesn't mistake it for ultimate reality, and of course everyone does until education or experience teaches you otherwise. Age is the season when "otherwise" catches up to you. Old people can make a marked contribution to general understanding if they will deal with their time insights realistically and boldly. Society of course conspires against their doing so. People say, "Mother is getting so forgetful" or "Grandfather recalls his entire boyhood but doesn't know what he had for lunch." And the younger people smile or weep or wring their hands. Are they so sure their own time-sense is superior, adhering to blips on a clock face or pages of a calendar? That word calendar, by the way, comes from the Latin for an account book, a ledger, and shows the passion for chronicling everything, making lists, keeping track. Where does it get others that old people have not got to? Maybe the old have a free hand with time that is not worthy of scorn but envy.

Years ago I knew a remarkable woman who had lived a long and adventurous life. She deliberately cultivated a dismissal of the past. She thought many people deteriorated because they were weighed down with memories. Like E. Graham Howe, the great British psychiatrist, she believed the key to living well was learning to die from every yesterday. When she was very old, she remembered the early years vividly, and unlike her family, I used to roam with her through those times—all in the present tense. I heard many marvelous tales about the world of grand opera and theater, Wall Street and politics; ocean liners, the Orient Express, London, Paris, Berlin. Oddly enough, she was constantly aware that I belonged to a different era, and would say things like, "You can't know that, you haven't even been born." After such a session, she would return to the present spontaneously and lucidly. She'd shake herself a little like a dog shedding rain, and smile. "All so long ago, but sometimes I wonder if it isn't still right here, if we just had eyes to see and ears to hear." To me that makes better sense than being shackled to one-directional time and very blamed righteous about it. How do we *know?* Only in the same way people once knew there was a flat earth. Totally present time seems contrary to common sense, but maybe that's only because the concept isn't that common yet. Nuclear physics still seems contrary to common sense to most of us, but more and more of our everyday lives is built on it.

Oh, I was forgetting the Dallas Cowboys, h'm? There is a medical doctor in Dallas named Larry Dossey who has written a book called *Space, Time and Medicine,* full of lovely infidel ideas about time. Dr. Dossey's concern with it is naturally medical, and he explores ways that linear time conduces to disease. He says the whole society suffers from "hurry sickness," owing to our being stuck in irretrievable time, which he finds a warped concept. When someone is sick, both patient and doctor are obsessed with time: How long has the disorder been going on? When will the pain cease? At what intervals shall the medication be given? When will morning come? What time is the doctor due? How much sleep is the patient getting? How fast or slow is the pulse? When can the patient go home? What is the usual duration of this disease? Critical illness is defined in terms of time running out.

Dr. Dossey regards this as unhealthy, defeating, irrelevant, focusing energy in the wrong direction. He reasons that the way we handle disease and the power to recover could be vastly improved by a different understanding of time, and he has conducted provocative experiments upon this premise.

The question is how to get the idea across to sick people in no shape to consider abstruse ideas remote from their immediate concern. Obviously, the more practical way is to undertake such pursuits in good health, and Dossey is constantly alert to methods of doing it. Living in the same city as the Dallas Cowboys, he soon heard of the professional athlete's peculiar relations to time, and he sought out team members for discussion.

A running back—in case you don't know (I didn't), that's one of the players who throws forward passes—told of seeing the complex movements of the game in slow motion. He watched his possible receivers working out their positions. He knew he had to get rid of the football in seconds, yet he experienced those seconds in an elongated form that let him quietly choose among the options before him. It was not merely *as if* time stretched out; it was actually present for him in that form.

A player on another team, a quarterback for the San Francisco Forty-Niners, echoed this experience. When he faded back to pass, he knew the opposing linemen were pounding down on him at speed, and he knew how big and determined they were, yet he too saw the interlacing patterns of the game in slow motion, as measured as a minuet or a symphony. He was aware that the whole thing appeared fast and heated to the people in the stands, but he was living in a larger time that enwrapped both the players and the onlookers. He wasn't ruled by their hurried view of the play.

Another of the Cowboys, a defensive end, had made a study of the exalted state known to all athletes when everything comes together—eye, body, mind, skill, the movements of the game—in one supple unit. The player knows precisely what is going to happen before it does, and he performs flawlessly.

That's the way they describe it afterward, but I think it is more accurate to say they know what will happen *concurrently* with its happening. They are after all not separate from the event; they don't just observe it, they are implemented into it. It feels like advance knowledge, but what is really taking place is a stepping outside of linear time into a simultaneity with pure time where events don't happen but simply are.

I say it because I have in my way sampled the phenomenon, and it is my contention that it happens to us all as one of the special faculties of aging, though I suppose one could contrive not to notice. I believe most young children experience it, but they don't yet understand its significance. It's a leftover from their antecedent existence and probably seems quite ordinary. Mystics and poets speak of such occurrences as otherworldly, a different kind of space, but it's my opinion that it's in this world all right, only enfolded in a different kind of time. It's having eyes to see and ears to hear, as my old friend said.

Obviously, I'm not a professional athlete, but the athlete is a human being, like me. He is not a freak or a superman. He draws only on principles available to all of us if we choose to utilize them. Gravity rules everything on earth, but some people use it in ways that can lift a space vehicle into orbit and bring it back. You can set a wheel in falling water and gravity will turn it over to generate electricity. Men balance gravity against the forces that resist it and raise a skyscraper fourteen hundred feet into the air. One can also use the perceived time changes of special fields to push back the walls of his own captivity in time.

One summer for reasons I won't detail here I had to walk over four miles under a blazing sun. Midway I began to lag. There wasn't any doubt of my continuing, but I had an incipient blister on one foot that felt like a shoe full of broken glass, I had an old-fashioned stitch in my side, and I was carrying a raincoat I had needed earlier in the day. I was tired, cross, and uncomfortable. I remembered reading about marathon runners, how they do not think ahead to the distance or time yet to go, but concentrate on the step they are making now, setting each foot down correctly, taking this breath evenly, refusing to consider whether they are gaining or losing on the clock.

I tried it, and it took discipline. My renegade mind *would* drift off again and again to the time-based questions, and I could see plainly that this was draining my energy and spoiling the present. I became intrigued with the mental process, and when the walk was finished, I was amazed. It wasn't nearly so late as I had expected, I wasn't exhausted, there was no pain, and I was even a little elated—my version of the runner's high.

I have since applied the principle when I am writing to a deadline or have too many tasks to do in one day, all equally necessary. I refuse to anticipate, but focus on the concrete now, this paragraph, this one plant to be cleared of weeds, this shirt to be ironed, book read, meeting planned. I've done a fair amount of work teaching people to use their creative abilities, and one of the most productive secrets I know is to treat each phase of a project as if that were the most important—which it is so long as it lasts, though maybe not in the overall picture.

You see this process in the meticulous care the Oriental flower arranger shows for the paper and string that wrap his flowers, or the monk's devotion to the lowliest job because it too is for the glory of God and therefore deserves respect. I never knew until recently that this is the same thing as regarding all time as equal, but that's what it is outside its linear strictures.

We forget that the events comprising our lives do not extend everywhere the same and thus that what we experience is not reality, but reality filtered through our perceptions. I can give you an example. A man I knew lay very ill in a New York hospital, and I was delegated by his oldest friend, who lived in California, to notify him of any change, day or night. The man died at two o'clock one morning and I at once made the phone call. Some years afterward the man from the coast and I were talking of those somber days, and he remarked in passing—he wasn't superstitious—that our friend had died on Friday the thirteenth. Much had been made by other people of his having died on his birthday, the fourteenth, and I was on the verge of correcting this man when I realized we were both right and both wrong.

Two A.M. in New York, when I had telephoned, was indeed eleven the previous night on the west coast. I was stunned and fascinated. Here was a miraculous thing: a man had died on two different days. Not just apparently, factually. What time he died from his own standpoint—if any—I cannot say.

Time is renewed every instant. And yet in the linear sense in which we mean it, there is no such thing as an instant. You cannot isolate a point small enough to qualify. Time has no duration. Past, present, and future are rough divisions we impose on time for obvious and practical reasons, but they are not real pieces of anything. We say today is the present, but the morning has already vanished, and tonight hasn't arrived. The first words of this sentence I am uttering have retreated into the past before I even come to its end.

The past exists only in memory, and—as in the case of my friend's death—a shaky, one-sided and variable memory it is. The future has yet to be invented. The present is a point of dissolution swifter than a nanosecond. What then can time be except wholly present—all the time?

I'm not recommending anarchy, for the love of heaven. Time is a form of ordering and order is indispensable if we are not to live in chaos. All I'm saying is loosen up about it. We are born into this world along with its time-scheme and must live in it. Nobody's going to escape that just by comprehending a larger time, any more than the sun ceases to rise and set just because we know we are the ones in motion. That knowledge allows us to move about in the earth, though, and now in the solar system. A wider comprehension of time enables one to come and go in that sphere in just the same way.

I can tell you very easily what it achieves: power, an old-fashioned thing called joy, above all, a heightened awareness that life is lived outside its visible limits. You want a prescription in one sentence? I haven't got one. But to be old is to have the solemnity of time constantly dented. It can begin to be noticeable in midlife, but never by the truly young because you can't have perspective without distance. I suppose everyone does different things with it, though. I find I slowly exchange time for tim*ing*—pace, rhythm, tempo in the musical sense—and that includes the rests, remember. Whoever writes the music puts in the silences as well. Without them, all he'd get is noise.

I now have a rebuttal to my old mother's nasty little verse: I call it redeeming the day. One can*not* throw minutes away—there's no place for them to go. Since time is not running out, I no longer have to build Rome in a day. A single good idea, one truth understood, one flash of beauty or sheer delight or laughter, one brief outpouring of faith or courtesy or skill makes that day worth living. When those days come in which nothing gets done and I have constant interruptions—or worse, I interrupt myself—I quietly seek out the one small particular that redeems the day: one line written, a poem read, a piece of music heard. I watch a sunset or fondle one of my animals or make a pie or converse with a friend or with God, and it is enough. Not infrequently it turns out that the squandering of time and the interruptions were necessary to the emergence of that satisfying fillip. That's not to say it's a rational design for all one's days. I repeat: we need time. We need the fixity and coordination it imposes. The only smart thing to do with a wasted day is to ride it like a wave. It too has something to teach. Robert Frost said some things have to be wasted to God. As with any external discipline, one masters time in all its moods in order to break through to the internal discipline—what I call timing, if you like—and then to go beyond both out into freedom. Nobody starts with freedom, though; one would not be able to handle it.

That's why most of this comes with age. A lot of life has to be lived to get where the old are. Santayana is much quoted these days for having said those who cannot remember the past are condemned to repeat it. I disagree, in part anyway. I don't think it is memory that releases us from repetition but the answer to this question: has one learned from the past? The principal goal is that our own experience shall not have been wasted on us. Then, and only then, can one dismiss the past and still retain one's identity. That's eerie but pleasant. Oh, nobody stays in unshackled time, not yet, but neither do you forget it. You can regain that timelessness at will, and it's at least as real as the chronological self and ten times more interesting.

Time is more wonderful to me now than ever. It's a natural resource. I love clocks and own a few elderly ones that I enjoy as works of art. I take a dim view of killing time. That's a mild but far from harmless kind of murder. It kills discernment, for one thing, and curiosity, command, vitality, response, humor, a number of other important elements.

People ask me now and then—they ask any writer, it's natural—how many hours I write at a sitting and whether I do it every day. I can't give them a proper answer because I no longer go at it that way. This embarrasses me as I believe in demystifying the arts. I'm responsible and besides, I like what I do, so I work at it seriously, but never to a predetermined level. I know it only when I reach it. It could be an hour, rarely less. I suppose three or four hours, usually, but I've been known to stick at it for sixteen. That's rare, too. A completed piece might take a day, a month, or a month of Sundays. It doesn't matter. The work shapes the time, not the other way around.

I don't wear a watch or own an alarm clock. I wake myself up if I need to. It's not that difficult; just don't take any nonsense from old habits. I can tell time by the sun or by shadows, or by my own inside if I'm hungry or sleepy. All old people know the phenomenon of being wide awake in the middle of the night. It's not insomnia, and taking pills only makes it worse or so my medical friends tell me. It's a natural manifestation of the fact that as we age, we need less sleep. It's a crime to waste it in restlessness and frustration. Mercy, it's like having a twenty-six-hour day. I usually read or listen to music—that wouldn't work if you have to worry about waking a household. But one could sew, cook, work out chess moves, carve wood—I knew one man who made handcrafted bows and arrows and sold them at a good price. I know another who does his ham radio bit—two A.M. is ideal for that. Why not write letters or update the stamp collection? My mother used to save the Sunday paper for her midnight reading through the week.

Time doesn't get shorter in age, it dissolves and is repossessed in a different context. Old people think it goes faster just because they can see around it, as one never can in youth. It's a privilege, not a punishment. Some of the new physicists say we live in a participatory universe; it is not "out there" at all. It takes its form and action, at least in part, from each one's own personal construction. Fifty years back the

American philosopher Ernest Hocking said the self is half of the world it experiences. Twenty centuries ago a man wrote, "Be not ignorant of this one thing, that one day is with the Lord as a thousand years, and a thousand years as one day." That gets brushed aside as poetry or wishful thinking, but it's only saying what I say and what's getting said in a lot of places—that time isn't linear but is everywhere present. We don't live in time, it lives in us. Sure we'll die—but if one dies old, the end of the road begins to look more and more like light at the end of the tunnel.

IV

THE OTHER SIDE OF LOVE

I'll talk about love but you won't like it. I said before that age is emancipation, and nowhere is that more true than in escaping the trammels of love. It takes gullibility to fall in love, and if one attains maturity along with growing old, one inevitably puts away childish things, gullibility included. Therefore one gets beyond love. And should. Oh, mercy, there I go making pronouncements. Why is that so seductive? Never mind, I know why, but we won't go into it now. So much guff is handed around about love and its alleged superiority to everything else that I get cross. I'd like to put a moratorium on the word for one solid year. We might learn something.

If it makes you any happier, I'll agree that there is such a thing as real love, and some thinkers try to differentiate between that and the popular sort by capitalization or quotation marks. The psychiatrist Howe always writes the good kind in small caps, LOVE, but I find the same word for two things confusing unless one already knows the distinction, in which case he doesn't need the diacritical nudging. Orally the two words are the same, and worst of all the concept of "real" love carries connotations of "my love is better than your love," which is demagoguery. I prefer to use other terms for the pure element—affection, compassion, charity, courtesy, there are many. As for love, I'll stick to the current corrupt usage. And to answer your question, yes, I am saying that it is not the greatest thing in the world.

Too many people go all their lifetime feeling defective or deprived because they have never known a great love; and think of the money poured down the drains of therapy trying to *make* it happen when the whole enchantment consists in the inability to make love do anything, come or go on command. Love beguiles us precisely because the human creature yearns to be swept away by an irresistible passion. A nasty streak of common sense warns us that other sorts of passion require serious work—discipline, courage, faith, study, even sacrifice. So does authentic affection, but in the razzle-dazzle of love that is easily ignored. One can always plead no talent in other fields, but erotic energy is rather widely distributed. It is congenial, flattering—because the race depends on it—and compelling enough to satisfy the yen for involvement with an elemental force.

But to expect oneself or another to continue at that stage is to invite doom. Which is about what we've got. It's crazy. It's asking a bolt from the blue to turn into a steady flame. You can no more swear to go on loving forever than you can to perpetuate any other feeling—joy, sorrow, anger, fear, excitement.

What most people call love was *invented* by troubadours in the twelfth century and never for a moment meant to be consummated in or out of marriage. By definition, consummation is the finish of something, the achievement of a goal, and thus the end of all that strives toward it. It's the journey's end. The troubadours knew that and were not about to sink their rapture in the quagmire of marriage or even a romp in the hay. To the contrary, they designed love as a solace for those necessary and somewhat sweaty functions. If that were kept in mind, marriage would be more satisfactory than it usually is and love affairs less harried and gloomed o'er with shadows.

Love is not the solution to anything, it's the problem. With a partner there are now two of you facing the problem, that's all. The best question I know for anyone contemplating marriage is whether the other person is one with whom you can foresee a decent, even pleasant life after love has dimmed, as it will. You can have love or truth but not both, and in the long run the human being wants truth more. In age one has got it—point blank and at some cost, but clear and earned. That is the crowning achievement in the end: to be one's own man or woman, to come back to being a self. Love can help, indeed yes. It's a challenging teacher, but don't mistake the teacher for the subject to be learned.

I don't know how to answer that usefully, but all

right, honesty is essential to this project; so yes, I have known two strong loves in my life. I count myself lucky; I'm not sure anyone has the right to such wonder twice. The first time I expected it, but not the second, which came in middle age. Oh, the latter by far. One has acquired a little realism by then that both heightens and tempers the delight. Now? I'm glad they happened and glad to have them behind me. It's all part of living and one does not regret one's own living, surely? It doesn't mean I'm wiser than someone else who only loved once or maybe never. It was just the road I needed to take. It seems to me the conclusions we reach in old age are often similar, however different the roads we travel. Those depend mainly on temperament. Somebody said—Voltaire maybe—that the man of imagination can discover in a day what takes the more literal-minded twenty years of hard experience.

What puzzles me, since we do so often come to like understanding, is why nobody levels with the young. Generation after generation we as a society go on pushing the same myths when we know—we must know if we have lived through them—that they are not true. I suppose it's tempting to cling to the hope that they could be true if enough people believed them. And then some people, especially parents, regard the young as a second chance to see their own dreams materialize. They think it is some flaw in themselves or plain bad luck that has made them come short of the promise. Others grow bitter and preach the emptiness of all human values, but that isn't true either. It only makes the young defiant to the point of anarchy which leads to bitterness in their own turn. And of course it is legendary that youth cannot imagine the old know beans about love, so it's not likely they would hear even if we did speak.

Probably the base reason for evasion, though—base in both senses, foundational and ignoble—is sentimentality, which is to say fuzzy thinking. I expect I am a voice crying in the wilderness since in 6,000 years nobody has succeeded in making thinking popular, but sentimentality is the worst pitfall of old age—of any time of life really, but in age utter disaster. It's gormless—you don't? it's British for what you'd call being a wimp—it has no class, it advertises to all and sundry that one has got through life without stirring his brain. Sentimentality is not great heart, it's an emotional binge about as deep as a salad plate. Not I, I can't make any such boast. It's tricky and wants a sharp lookout. That much I aim to do.

Very well, I can name several. We don't tell them that love is selfish. Ideally I suppose it can be mutually selfish, but that doesn't elevate it much. The body has legitimate hungers that strike magic in the affections, but even when the other body has a matching appetite, love is bent on its own gratification, as it has to be. Nobody else can eat for us, or breathe or laugh or cry in our stead. I'm not saying love is evil; it's often glorious, but it is not the magnanimity it is claimed to be and no amount of hyperbole will make it so. It certainly adds spice. Salt savors food, and meat and bread are flat without it. But one cannot live on salt.

Soon after I was divorced, a young actor came to

see me. I was forty-two, he was twenty-seven. We had met twice at the home of a theatrical producer and I thought he might be interested in a script of mine that had been discussed. Instead he made me a proposition—open, endearing, complimentary except that I was too flabbergasted to be flattered. A bit at sea, I reminded him that he was married, the father of an infant daughter. He asked if that offended me and I said no, but it might well offend his wife. He replied that he had not supposed marriage was at issue on either side, and he was of course correct. I then pointed out that I was fifteen years his senior. He wanted to know if I found that a barrier. Not exactly, but it threw me out of context. At his age I would have thought a woman my age was over the hill. He laughed aloud at that.

I finally said I had just ended a long marriage, which he knew, and was not at all sure what I wanted next. It was not my way to rush into any action as a means of finding out.

"All right," he agreed, "I accept that. I can even understand it a little. But I will hope to change your mind." He smiled. "In time." Then he added the only false note. "I only want you to be happy."

There was a time when that would have sounded tender, but I knew it was false because of the age difference. I had lived long enough, as he had not, to know that we believe what we want to believe. We imagine love can be unselfish.

He stayed for coffee and we talked of many things: men and women, ideas, talent, modern society, ambition. As he was leaving he said, "I wasn't honest, was I, when I said I wanted your happiness? I want my own. My old parish priest tried to tell me that a dozen years ago, and I didn't know what he was talking about. Maybe I'm beginning to."

I told him if he kept on like that he'd probably be a fine actor one day. I thought myself very wise and cool, seeing to it that nobody got hurt, but the truth is I could afford to be unselfish. *My* sensibilities were not at risk.

Take the myth that all the world loves a lover. False. Oh, people may smile on lovers, the way they smile on a toddler who has just learned to ride a tricycle and is as pleased as a dog with two tails, but such tolerance is brief. Love is a wild horse, and society does everything in its power to break it to harness. The world cannot abide love. As C.S. Lewis once said, whether a man is allotted one wife or four, in *no* society can he have just any woman he fancies.

Have you never noticed when lovers marry how often the whole thing falls apart? They move from one medium to another and naively expect everything to stay as it was. Some friends of mine had an unusually happy affair—in so far as a third person can know—and I tried to talk them out of marriage. Not gratuitously; they asked me, but that kind of advice is never actually wanted and I shan't do it again. At all events, after tearing up a good deal of turf on both sides they did marry, and it lasted two months.

What lovers will never accept is that they are not unique nor do they live in a vacuum. Even a hermit in the desert has a setting, and lovers live like anybody else surrounded by circumstances that largely gave rise to their love and largely sustain it. Change the setting and you have a very different affair on your hands—or none at all. It's like an eddy in water. It may be as powerful as a maelstrom, but that doesn't make it any less subject to the winds and currents that swirled it into being.

I know one couple—*one*—who handled the transition from lovers to spouses with intelligence and success. He was married, she not, when they fell in love. He was a government official, she had a prosperous career, and the divorce laws in their country were strict. After a few years of delight, anguish, partings that did not last, they recognized that *they* were corroding something wonderful. As the woman said to me later, they were hopeless amateurs, which was witty because the word also means lovers.

They cared enough to come to terms with their situation as it was. They made sensible arrangements—financially, socially, professionally—and lived within them. It was not always easy, but what life is? Her apartment became a second home for him, but it remained hers; she paid for it, he never took it for granted. She accepted invitations for holidays and other occasions when he was obligated elsewhere. Recriminations were taboo. They traveled widely, always accompanied by a woman friend who tactfully disappeared at intervals. They were lucky in her—and she in them: they paid part of her expenses and showed her a world not otherwise available to her.

Suddenly circumstances changed, through no action of their own, and they were free to wed. They were by turns incredulous, pleased, and alarmed. For twenty years they had lived on a plan affording them riches few marriages attain: fresh stimulus, new friends and ideas, constant input from the outside world. To alter that and not damage the relationship was impossible. Once again they made reasonable plans, deliberately incorporating the old status into the new.

They share a house, but each has a semiprivate suite. They maintain their careers which necessitates their being apart occasionally and means that each continues to see people the other does not know. They travel without a companion now, but frequently to different cities on business, meeting later at a third city in the earlier pattern of enforced discretion.

That kind of thing takes money, I agree, but they earn it as they always did. The love most people want and think they've got till they find out it doesn't just happen takes effort, thought, sacrifice. It takes common sense, which is maybe the rarest thing of all. Age helps. At twenty, one marries in the belief that you can make another person your own. At fifty, one knows that isn't possible—or desirable. Nobody can *have* another human being, as slave owners find out, not even if you both want it that way. Nature will spit in your eye.

And that's another myth, that love equates with possession. We do it constantly with things: if you're crazy about something, buy it. That's one reason possession doesn't work with people: it turns a person into an object. Sooner or later the healthy soul rebels. Twice I have loved a painting with an unreasoning passion to own it. One was a Rembrandt, the other by Cézanne. I didn't want much, did I? Each was hanging on a museum wall, and I would never in a thousand years acquire them. Of course I knew, but that didn't stop me. Hollywood would buy one of my stories; they would find oil on our old family ranch; someone would make me an heiress.

What woke me up was not the wildness of my scheme but its self-contradiction. I returned to the museums now and then to wallow in my enchantment, and one day as a tour group bustled past me bent on the lunchroom, not even glancing at my love, I suddenly saw my folly. Nobody owns a painting, only the wall behind it. Either those pictures were already mine in every sense that matters or they were mere blobs of color on canvas. Art belongs to those who have eyes to see. It belonged to the artist once but he lets it go, because that's why he created it and otherwise it dies.

But try that on with a person. Have you ever loved enough to let go, to give up what you think has to happen, for the sake of another's destiny? Nor I, except once when I had no choice, and that doesn't count. That's like easing my young actor out of his infatuation when I didn't care that much. I'm talking about letting go *because* you love, about nonpossession. In age it at least becomes comprehensible. However much one is drawn to thinking otherwise, one has to admit that no love is world-shattering. "I can't live without you" sounds rather grand, but you can, and you will enjoy it if you've got it in you, and if you haven't, nobody else would have made the slightest difference.

I told you you wouldn't like it. Look around. Lasting marriages are mostly accomplished by the dominance of the wife and the dependence of the husband. Men may want wives but they need mothers, and most women are born nurturers. Historically if nothing else. They're getting weary of it and marriage is in a state of unrest, but that's another problem.

It isn't only erotic love that suffers from myth. The parent-child bond is unbelievably romantic. Not so much the other way because nature provides in growing up that the child shall revolt, and in doing so he discovers his parents are just people. It is right there that authentic friendship, even affection, could be established but parents are constitutionally incapable of seeing children as anything but adjuncts. And for all their clear-sightedness the children will do the same when they become parents. Not because they love; because they don't think. Love is supposed to obviate thinking.

Some do. A man I knew was offered in midlife one of those phenomenal breaks in one's career, a chance he had long hoped for. It would mean his being away for six months of the year, and he had one child still in high school, an only daughter whom he adored. She was quiet, sensitive, and somewhat of a misfit in a swinging society. He felt she needed him acutely just then to make the shift from girl to woman, and he turned down the job offer.

His efforts to help the girl were not welcome. She finally said, "Dad, I know I'm not like other kids, but I'm okay. Oh, I might like some more dates and stuff, but they'd have to be *with* somebody. I mean, I'd have to like the guy, do you see?" He saw, and backed off and watched her evolve her own way.

She was a good student and won a scholarship to college where she met a young engineer much like herself and married him. She went on to an outstanding career with an oil company, as well as raising two children.

"She's a whiz," her father said. "Still quiet, still rather plain in a curiously beautiful way, if that makes sense. I've wondered many times if she ever needed me the way I planned, or whether I was using her because I was afraid of the big jump. I'll never know, but I'll tell you this: I respect her. We have a very nice thing going between us."

There cannot be much doubt that he loved her—enough to be honest with himself, and that's what's missing in most parental love, in all romantic love. But was the choice he made the right one for him? Is love ever the all-purpose solution it is purported to be?

Another parent who faced up to sentimentality was Ralph Waldo Emerson. He wanted a son more than anything in life, and when at last one was born to him he was overcome by joy. His one terror was that something might happen to the child—in those days things did. When the little boy was five, he died of pneumonia, and for Emerson there was neither sun nor moon. He wrote in his journal that all he believed had failed, life could never again have meaning. Yet two years later he was recording zest and happiness in his work, in his wife and family, in his social life—and it shocked him. Was he betraying his son? Was he a shallow man, incapable of true feeling? Scholar that he was, he examined the phenomenon strictly and concluded that all emotion is by nature not unreal but transitory. One can no more preserve it in its initial purity than one can shut up a sunset in a box to be opened and re-experienced on another day. Somehow we must learn that to taste an emotion in its fullness is to have known it entire.

A woman whose marriage had been an exceptional one for forty years—again, speaking as an outsider—lost her husband in severe wartime conditions; they both had been imprisoned. One day over tea I asked her how she had managed to accept his death, for she was plainly enjoying life. She replied slowly, "I don't know of course whether we shall ever meet again, but that man taught me how to live and I'm not going to behave now in a manner he would detest. And if I do see him again someday, would you want me to have nothing to say?" In twenty years I never heard that woman use the word love. She didn't have to.

Love is a tyrant, but do we say so? Almost as if it knew its own fragility, love demands the exclusion of whatever does not pertain directly to itself. Wives habitually regard a man's work as a threat—most would rather cope with another woman any day. Men who insist they work only for the wife and kiddies are either mouthing a socially acceptable myth or trying to get their wives off their backs. As women more and more seek their own interests, that is changing, but it will be a long time before any large segment of them find in work the identity that men do. Probably never so long as they cling to romantic love.

Our forebears were not wrong to put work, duty, religion, family, social service, and other obligations ahead of love in the scale of worth. They weren't ignorant or heartless, they knew life has to have some structure and love isn't it. In Bible times a man newly wed was exempt from civic duties including military service for one year. Like mourning, which says a lot about both moods. After that he was expected to return to normal living. In Dante's poem, you may recall, the love-blinded lovers who stay that way wind up in hell.

The present fashion of flinging oneself into sundry beds in the belief that one will prove to be the "right" answer is pathetic. How can you expect commitment, to say nothing of loveliness or wonder, from someone who plows across a singles bar and introduces himself—or increasingly herself—by saying, "Your place or mine?"

That isn't clear-eyed and realistic; it's more insanely romantic than any amount of hearts and flowers. Isolated sexuality is tasteless, but it doesn't concern me so much as the addled idea that every random coupling is love and potentially the answer to life's profoundest questions. Under the happily-ever-after approach was a bedrock recognition of the long haul. Today's young people accept only bed, and they don't understand that. Listen to their talk—and oh mercy, how they do talk. In catchwords and slogans. They prattle of loving and caring, warm, giving, openness, meaningful, sharing, never, and forever. They define and describe and analyze and repeat and repeat to cover the blankness of raw grabbings. Like Maupassant's little Breton girl who was raped and afterwards kissed her attacker's forehead in an effort to make some beauty to remember.

This generation calls any sexual exploit "making love" as if sex substantiates and informs love, rather than the reverse. This makes both sex and love into a kind of war game. Two hundred years ago "making love" was the opposite of explicit. It was used in genteel society by both men and women to mean flirting, grace notes on what is otherwise a not very pretty human activity. I don't know a modern word for it. I doubt there is one; nobody bothers with nuances.

I'm inclined to believe that the deepest need of human beings is to be important. It's not cheap; it is the ages-long cry for meaning, that life shall have some purpose. Love bestows a momentary sense of having found it because we confuse private urgency with external greatness. Love makes us feel important but it has no importance of itself, outside narrow limits.

There's a recurring theme in the writings of Enid Bagnold that has always intrigued me. In several of her plays and novels a husband suddenly announces after thirty years or so that there is something missing from his life and he is leaving to search for it. One notable aspect is that it is the man who feels this restlessness. All my life it has been assumed to be woman's peculiar property. The wife in the story is stunned, angry, embarrassed, and sometimes heartbroken, but she soon finds that her own life has been lacking a long-forgotten value—a singular self, that one-to-one intensity with which we first face the world and find it good.

Miss Bagnold was too sophisticated to offer solutions for either partner, but she knew the questions have to be asked and that they ask themselves after a certain age, though of course one can duck them. In age you realize, even if you don't admit, that the critical relationship has always been with yourself.

If I suggest that love is good for nothing, I'm doing something wrong. Without feelings nothing gets done, but without intellect the wrong things get done. We must go through love if we would grow up, and the operative word is *through*, the necessary passage to the far side of anything. What age teaches, even insists, is that love has a far side, and a good thing, too. Anything that goes on forever is shapeless, tedious, and loses its point. Like an endless novel or symphony, a painting without edges or a never finished summer or war.

Ah, yes, but eternal life is another fantasy, and it would take a good deal of reschooling to make it palatable. Physiological survival is not living. When all one's energies are spent in avoiding death, one has already lost the vital factor. Life is the ground but not the content of itself. But love is commonly expected to be just that: its own cause and effect, its own reason for being.

Like it or not, we are designed whole but we are born subjective and that makes us lopsided. Love is good in that it takes us somewhat out of ourselves but bad if at some point it fails to give us back. Both experiences—falling in love and outgrowing it—

contribute to our objectivity, which is essential if we are to learn what is true. It is not love alone that one gets beyond but all emotion—no, say better emotionalism. Old people have strong feelings, maybe deeper than ever, but one is no longer a slave to them. Age brings proportion, the long view, which is poise. Life is neither subjective nor objective but both in precise balance. Extremely so; no wonder it takes a lifetime to get the hang of it.

V

THE RESILIENT MIND

Old age is like a fortune cookie: nobody takes it very seriously, but everybody wants to know what is written there. I have yet to see anyone toss aside the little scrap of paper without reading it. The last cookie I opened said, "Flee fornication." I ask you. I showed it to my dinner companion and remarked, " 'The wicked flee when no man pursueth.' " It gave us a good laugh, and there could be worse fortunes.

Few people honestly believe age has much to add to life, but most of us don't exactly wish to have it cut short. It's hard to shake a pervasive sense that there's something waiting in the wings for its chance. That something is mind. Pushed aside through the long years of business and family, of earning and housing and feeding and clothing, the mind in age asserts itself with unsinkable aplomb. Minds are amazing stuff. They can lie dormant for years, and then, given the slightest attention, emerge as fresh as the dawn.

Age is the ideal time for it. One of the worst mistakes we make in educating children is that we constantly give answers to questions their minds haven't yet asked. That's why many people remember so little of their schooling. In age one is awash with questions, and what the mind really desires to know, it will find out and retain. Sometimes I marvel that children learn as much as they do; they were never designed to sit still in classrooms for five hours a day. The old sit still very ably. As the outer world of action smalls down, the inner universe of intellectual interest erupts like the fairytale beanstalk, the top of which disappeared into the sky. After sixty, one has what no youngster can possibly have—the necessary field experience to transpose education into intuition.

By education I don't mean schooling, though I don't not mean it either. The mind needs some tools. The winter of life is an education in itself, but not if you don't know what you're looking at, as the Vikings did not know when they saw America five hundred years before Columbus. What one gets from school if one is lucky, even from four undergraduate years of college, is learning *how* to learn, the means with which to think. Thinking itself is a delayed skill; most of our lives things merely flutter through our minds. Thinking begins only when habit fails, and, believe me, in old age habits come crashing down right and left. Nothing fits, nothing works any more. One can of course retreat into self-protection but it's better fun to think.

I *know* what statistics show about declining mental agility and depleted faculties, but statistics are dead; I'm living. There is a point we must get straight before we go any farther: statistics are not real things and they are not causal. As I said about the odds on getting sick, one may indeed fall ill and that can be numerically measured, but the odds will not have *caused* it. The fact that two and two is four does not in itself improve my bank balance. If you have ten dollars and I have five, the average between us is $7.50, but no one body, no living human being, exists in our little group of two who manifests the average. So it is with powers and IQs and the chances of getting married.

Statistics are a convenient fiction for handling large masses of detail, for surveying and summarizing, but as a guide to living they are useless and often a lie. Life does not come as theory upon which we hang experience but just the opposite—life comes as experience from which, if you insist, theories can be distilled. Life is lived by one lone statistically insignificant mortal at a time—do people really have to be told that? Without you and me living our singular and undiagramed lives, statistics would suffocate for want of input. Let the statistics adapt to us, that's their job; even as it's our job to put a dent in them. You don't have to agree with me; you only need to know, as my young friends put it, where I am coming from.

I could very nearly give you a formula for living old in two words: learn something. But watch out—that's not as facile as it sounds. A mind in motion tends to remain in motion, and there is no top on learning—like my beanstalk. That's an advantage in learning late. By that time one knows one is never going to figure out everything. Old people don't want life solved, they want it lived.

Along the same line, the old have abandoned fame, even small local fame. They not only don't expect acclaim for learning, they are suspicious of it. Outside recognition, even if it comes, is no match for the inner recognition one gives oneself. If you know a thing, it is known in the universe, and that's enough.

Then, too, there is the lack of cocksureness. Like the King of Siam in the Rodgers and Hammerstein musical about him, one is not sure at all of what once was known absolutely. Conclusions made long ago don't stay concluded. And like the king, one becomes receptive to fresh ideas, kicking and yelling a little no doubt, but still open. One no longer insists upon insistence. It's dizzying but gratifying.

In the latter days there is an absence of noise, which is an aid to concentration, and an awareness that no amount of education will transform one from a pumpkin into a golden coach. It is an adolescent delusion to imagine that, say, expensive clothes will cause the world to appreciate one's true worth. A certain literary critic said that after fifty he discovered a man didn't really need more than two suits: one to wear, one at the cleaner's. So, too, the grown-up student goes at education differently from the young. The child asks what the letters of a word spell. The adult wants to know the meaning and supposes he has got it solidly. The old learner seeks variations in the meaning, turns the word over and over like a stone or a shell to find its secret shape and texture, the colors, the heft of it in his mind.

Above all, the old make good learners because they can abide truth. They don't mind that it isn't always to their liking. They like it for being itself, and on that basis they find ways of coming into congruence with it. The late decades are when inner growth comes into its own. The mind sheds skin like a snake in spring, and there's the design standing out fresh and clear. That's what education is: learning to see connectedness, how things fit together to make pattern, color, sense. That takes detachment and stillness, both assets that require long cooking. All my life I've heard people exclaim, "Oh, if I'd known at twenty what I know now!" and that's crazy talk. Nobody's forty-five at twenty-one; they mutually exclude each other. The notion that we can somehow learn all we need to know at an early age and reap the benefits ever after is fool's gold. Even if you could do it, it wouldn't satisfy. Living *is* learning, which is another way of saying that life is successive—and vincible—ignorances. For forty years I thought myself a reasonably knowledgeable person, and I worked at it, but now I wonder if I knew much of anything before sixty. If I'm lucky and keep working at it, I expect to say the same at eighty.

The great Japanese printmaker Hokosai studied his art assiduously from the age of seven. When he was seventy-five he said he had been woefully ignorant until he was seventy. At eighty-five he would hope to have learned a little more. By ninety he might deserve to be called an artist. At one hundred ten, if he got so far—ah, then every line he put on paper would be worth something. That cheers me. The whole purpose of living is to learn, and that purpose does not fade. The crux is to keep on with it. There are levels of understanding appropriate to every age. Full inner growth comes late, that's all.

There was an old villager in England who enrolled in their post-war adult education program at one of the so called red-brick colleges. When at ninety-one he obtained his degree, reporters flocked around to ask what he'd got it for. "Why, for me," he said in surprise. "I can't think who else. Education tells you where you fit into the world. It's what my old dad called bein' me own man."

I love that. Education "takes" in the old as it seldom does in youth because they have no need to wring secondary gains from it. They aren't trying to get anything out of it except the heady skill of being their own masters, and that's what education is really about. In Enid Bagnold's play *The Chinese Prime Minister* the seventy-year-old heroine exclaims, "There is a me in me I haven't conquered yet—or even found!" It's only when one can acknowledge that, and like the idea, that education is seen for what it is, a continuous self-evolving.

Some kind of instruction is more or less necessary at first, or else one has to formulate one's own plan and that takes a considerable skill. I know I said self-education is the end, but it's rarely the beginning. Depends upon how much formal training one has had in the past. I once lamented to a professor at Columbia Teachers College that I'd done far more studying after college than I ever did in, and he said calmly, "Then your university did a good job. That's what you're there for—to develop a lifelong taste for it."

There's a flip side to systematic study that isn't so nice. People can fall in love with it and mistake it for the real thing, running around forever taking courses. Somewhere along the way one must quit getting ready—for anything—and just do it.

But look here: I do not suggest everyone is a closet genius. I do say anybody can learn anything at any age—*enough,* that is to say, in some fashion that is satisfying and honest. All right, it's extravagant, but so's a sunrise. We don't really know how people learn, only that they do, and there is no evidence to show the capacity shuts off at some point. It's like the pyramids and standing stones. It's not known how they got there, either, but there they are, mysteries so profound they exude a magnetic field felt by anyone who comes within range. The resilient mind is no less electrifying.

I urge a modest foray into systematic study because it is more direct than flubbing around on one's own, and because it yields four fundamentals. First, focus—the realization that education is learning that goes someplace, not a grab bag. Second, input—it is really rather difficult to have ideas without information; one discovers how to go and get it. Third, discipline—the catching and refining of innate powers, not unlike what an athlete does. And fourth, familiarity with mind as a talent—the recognition that one can choose the mind's occupations and by so choosing command one's events and conditions. Command, I said, not dictate.

Some months back I needed some information about the making of silk for a story I was writing. I knew it began with a caterpillar and finished on a loom, and in between nothing. I soon got involved with French history—about which I was almost as ignorant—because France had been silk merchant to the western world for two hundred years. I found Louis XIV repeatedly referred to as the Sun King, without explanation; apparently any half-educated reader should know. I was nettled, and when I finished with my silk inquiry, I borrowed a biography of Louis. It turned out he was born to a childless royal couple twenty-three years after their marriage, and as France sorely needed an heir to the throne, the child's birth seemed to the whole nation like a sunlighted miracle. Louis thought so too and spent a lifetime decking himself and his court with glitter.

As is common with any new bit of information, I then stumbled upon the Sun King at every turn—flipping through an art magazine, a travel book lying on somebody's coffee table, a conversation heard at dinner—and I was entranced to be in the know, versed in one small corner of general knowledge. Like my English villager, I was by that fraction more at home in my world.

That's another thing education is: a growing awareness of the situation one is in. A certain degree of that is thrust upon one as one grows old, but randomness doesn't satisfy. One yearns to pull a few things together. It need not, probably should not, be heavily academic. Reading a book will serve to start with, if it catches your interest, and for the love of heaven choose an area that does engage you. If you try to find out things you really don't care to know, you'll be bored out of your skull, and they won't stay in your mind twenty minutes. Curiosity is all. Education is gossip made respectable.

Learning always begins along some line, but it doesn't stay there. One way to tell that the real thing is happening to you is when a hundred tantalizing side-roads lead off in all directions. One cannot follow them all and has to make choices, but that's a small price to pay for treasure at the end. Of course, it never does quite end, and one discovers he will never be done with finding things out. Once you know that, you have got the heart of the matter and I wish you Godspeed. Welcome to infinity.

Pick up a second book leading off from the first one and you will never be the same. People sense that; it's why the idea of education has a scary side, but one goes through being scared to having more of oneself. There's a me in everyone not previously met, but—oh, my—hankered for. Any librarian will help compile a decent reading list for the asking. Or a retired teacher if there is one handy. My town has lots, and they are always ready to explore, advise, scold a little. I suppose it's native to the grain.

A good alternate starting point is to take a correspondence course—from a reliable school, not a bucket shop promising fame and fast money. You'd be surprised; the country's a hive of decent schools and colleges with community education programs. Harvard's got one, and they call its students "non-traditional," a medieval term I think. It would be. They range from fifty-five to ninety-three and from bellhops to corporate executives and congressmen.

Of course if one lives nearby one can always attend classes. Some people are lonely and profit from the company, which is legitimate but a slightly different proposition. Me, I like doing it by mail.

Two reasons. For one thing, it's more intimate, oddly enough. Here again, it varies with one's prior experience, but one really does outgrow classrooms. Correspondence is more like a tutorial where one is alone with the instructor, the most intensive and rapid way of learning. A professional teacher is someone who will quarrel with you on the level of reasoned ideas, and that isn't feasible in groups.

I sometimes take a correspondence course in winter, usually something apart from my own field, but one year it was one-act playwriting, a thing I fiddle with as an amateur. It wouldn't hurt to learn a little about what I was doing. Every time the mail brought back an assignment the professor had corrected, shredding my efforts—and my ego—to ribbons, I would pace the floor for three days arguing furiously. What did that professor know; he was a *teacher*, not a writer (precisely, but I could not yet allow myself the luxury of that). How dare he find fault with my brilliant ideas? What he suggested was tedious, clumsy, dramatically flat, and anyway impossible. I even sank to the shameful charge that he was young enough to be my son—I didn't know that, but it seemed likely.

Then the mean facts would surface that I was wasting time and had paid out $130, and I would sit down and write, determined that it should not work. After a page or so, I knew it would; at midpoint I was excited; in the end I was smug. See what a clever student I was. In two weeks the whole thing would happen again. I sometimes suspected that man of provoking me on purpose to get more juice into my work, but what I got into my head was some comprehension of playwriting, and how he managed this was his affair.

That sort of result seldom follows from reading a book, not until one gets experienced; it is too easy just to put the book down. Nobody holds you to it during the angry time, or drives you to see that you are angry at the wrong thing but that anger itself is a useful energy. Nor does it happen in a room with thirty other people. The element of hand-to-hand combat is lacking. In education one wrestles with a single angel, not an army.

My second reason for ranking written study higher than classwork is just that—that it's written. Every least idea, comment, or question has to be captured in words on paper, and I'm not sure that isn't the whole key to learning just as it stands. It serves anyway as another definition of what education is: the art of lucid statement. That legendary child who is supposed to have asked, "How can I know what I think till I see what I say?" wasn't all that foolish.

I had a friend in her eighties who was more or less housebound and despairing. I asked her to help me in a project. She was to learn five new words a week—only that. But she had to read something, at least the daily paper, or listen to broadcasts just to encounter new words. At first she depended on me to check them out in my dictionary, but then she wanted one of her own. It was heavy enough to merit a small separate table, and she had to get out of her chair to consult it. She was gleeful when she stumped me, and we quarreled amiably over derivations and usages. And constantly marveled at the mystery of language: which comes first, mind or speech?

One day she told me she was going to take up an old pursuit, the study of a foreign language. She was already fluent in French and German, which she had been taught in childhood; now she would add Italian—and she did. At last she said, "You did it deliberately, didn't you, to wake me up?" I said yes but not as therapy. It was an honest bit of research for my work.

An old saying has it that a little learning is a dangerous thing, owing to the human tendency to get puffed up. But sayings are never the whole story; they are too severely edited, which is what makes them sayings. For every true proverb there is a contrary one just as pithy. A little learning is also a fecund thing. Education nourishes itself and overflows like the Nile, turning the driest desert green.

To own five words free and clear in all their color and nuance and swiftness is simply to become human. Language is the primal factor that sets us apart from the rest of creation. The whole industrio-techno-commercial civilization hangs on it absolutely. Oh yes, including math. "Two plus two equals four" is a sentence, after all, and so are all its cousins and its aunts. Numbers are a shorthand for words, or a different alphabet if you like. And words are a shorthand for ideas of infinite number and subtlety and complexity.

Oh, mercy, ask me something easy. Nobody knows how language began. It's possible it never did—not as something added on after we got here; we were verbal from the beginning. I'm inclined to think so, since it is plain that mind and speech are correlates, each existing in reciprocity to the other. An Old Testament writer remarks that God set the whole world in men's hearts so that they cannot find it out from the beginning to the end. As the eye sees everything except itself, which it can never see, so it takes language to discern language and we cannot disentangle it because we cannot disassemble ourselves.

If a little learning is dangerous, a lot is a catastrophe. I would not weigh everyone down with scholarship; I merely say a brain is an unsinkable natural resource. Where the body turns cranky and stubborn, the mind remains supple—alive, nosy, full of intrigue and enchantment. I would say to all human beings, "You got talent, kid; use it." Education is largely willing attention, and one can pay heed to the ceiling overhead in a nursing home if that's all his present scope—the color and texture of the plaster, a crack that forms a design, a spider that has somehow got up there and how did she do that? Take one small particle of living and expand it, breathe on it as the creator in Genesis breathed on man. You think you know what it is to see and hear, but do you really? How long is it since you consciously savored your senses with pride, glee, wonder? Most people give it up around age three, not from choice but because the world is vast and to cope with it requires a certain homogenization. In age one reawakens to one's own smallness and to the greatness of that smallness. The most creative periods in history were enacted on very small stages—Athens in the fifth century B.C., Renaissance Italy, Shakespeare's London, colonial America.

Five years ago I set myself to increase the use of my left hand, even to writing with it a little. It's not pretty but it's legible. The following summer I painted the entire interior of my house, and you've no idea what a boon it is to be able to wield a paintbrush lefthandedly in tight corners. Or to switch over when the right arm tires in mixing cookies or pulling weeds or ironing clothes. The hardest thing is using scissors, but I can do that too if I go slow.

I did it because it struck me as a neglected resource, but what it did to my mind astonished me. I am told that art students are sometimes put to drawing with their left hands, not to become proficient but because it jostles them into new vision, and so it was with me. The left hand is the dreamer, the poet, the prophet, and the whole process thrust me back into a novice relation with the world. The child I once was was not dead, not vanished. I not only remembered, I lived her again. But now my taller self could see farther, had patience with small progress, knew better where we were going, how to make choices—and the two selves fused into a new identity, or else a very old one long sought.

It doesn't need explaining; that's part of the accomplishment and the joy. In age these things just happen; one drops theorizing for being. Education allures and sticks because it has ceased to be an obligation. The impulse arises from within, which is the ideal precondition but almost impossible to instill from without, though obviously teachers and parents are reduced to attempting it. In fact, to induce free will is a contradiction in terms. Ultimately one has to get there on his own. Examples can help, very little else.

Motor skills are supposed to be harder for old people to master than intellectual ones. Understandable, but I'm not sure it's wholly true, either. A friend who is a ski instructor says that beginners in their fifties are by no means rare and are among his most apt pupils. I know one woman who learned at sixty-five and skis happily ten years later. A woman in my neighborhood got her first driver's license at sixty-four and has had it steadily renewed for eighteen years. I myself learned to ride a bicycle at fifty very quickly and without one fall because my adult mind told me that safety on a two-wheeled vehicle lay in maintaining speed. I learned to play the piano even later; I'm no Rubinstein but it's recognizable music and it gives me pleasure.

It's wicked to tell people they cannot learn, whatever the rationale. Without morale, one hasn't got a chance. Long ago I did some work with one of the world's great literacy teachers. He showed me a memorable photograph of an old Nubian standing tall and proud under the Egyptian sun, holding out between his two hands a book from which he was reading. He had been told all his life that he could never read because his head was the wrong shape, a fact he could see for himself; he had a long skull like an El Greco painting, and this sounded rational and "scientific" to him. The visiting instructor taught him to read in two months. Sometimes when I am low in my mind, I think of that Egyptian, clad in rags but wearing a fierce aristocracy because he could read—and I go on.

If the old are slow and uneasy about tackling new ideas, it may be that they were wrongly taught in the first place and not that their minds are crumbling. Everybody's taught wrong in a measure because we are taught by human beings no better and no worse than us, who did not themselves have all the answers. Neither have we, of course, and the only honorable stand any imparter of knowledge can take is to remember that no knowledge is fixed.

In the vintage years one has learned better than to demand of life what it has not got and never had to give—namely, absolute certainty. That's if one is not scared off by self-appointed authorities who insist a lack of being very damn sure what's what is a sign of senility. That's twaddle. It's a special aptitude found in the old and more or less closed off to others—a particular openness to intuition, metaphor, meaning. This whole existence may well be a metaphor but show me anybody young who will face up to that without blinking. Not all the old do it either, of course, but that's primarily because they're brainwashed; otherwise it's a natural bent.

The trouble with language is its litmus-paper superiority. It is so explicit and dazzling that it makes us trash the implicit and subtler elements of learning—insight, mood, gesture, the sensual fabric of life which we madly reduce to eroticism; wonder, religion, poetry, myth; the lightning bolt of unarticled knowing. The language that has given us power over the rest of creation has also bereaved us of the ways in which we are integrated into it, and the soul goes hungry and weeps.

But in age all the old inklings and affinities and

bearings come flooding back. A lifetime of schemes and undertakings have humbled one to see and taste again the initial goodness. I'm not trying to get rid of language—I'd be out of a job if nothing else, and education would be impossible. We are born trailing clouds of glory and lose them primarily because infants have no speech. They don't *know* what it is they've got. *Intuition* too is a word, and so is *blue*, so is *love*. Without words and their strict pruning, we too easily drift back to the superstition and sentimentality against which science was so largely a rebellion. Oh, yes, and a salvation, without a doubt.

The big middle of life is not wrong or bad or wasted, it is just not the apex. There is more to come, and one needs to carry into that "more" all the precision acquired in the language-based years, while yet keeping open house to the nonverbal promptings of this new phase, which have their own secrets. The basic fact is that we have two ways of knowing, even as we have two hands and eyes and halves of brain. It is a terrible mistake to isolate them from one another. They are meant to work in union, and together they form an ability that neither has alone.

I used to work for a savvy and dictatorial editor who would often say, "A good hunch is worth any amount of hard facts." He was talking about writing, but the practice of any art is only a sort of being old before one's time. Artists are compelled early to trust what is happening, even when it's absurd. They're not smart, they just have no choice. I hear a lot of talk about a coming post-modern era. Well, one is already post-modern when one is old, and there is a kind of giddy glory in trusting the process.

Age is a minor earthquake, a slippage in the crust when the whole scale of values shifts. It's not a reason to panic. In Aeschylus's play *Agamemnon*, the old king says, "I hold my own mind, and think apart from other men." Now is the time for it. The pertinent question is not, "How can I get back to what I was a few years ago?" but "What has this got to teach me? What can I learn?"

VI

THE SPINNING WHEEL

When I was engaged full-time in the world of publishing, broadcasting, and theater, with a splash of politics, I often heard the lament, "Why can't I be liked for what I am, and not for what I do?" It's pure humbug. For one thing, the dwellers in such regions *eat* admiration for their endeavors and would die of malnutrition in a week without wads of it. And more to the point, a self *is* what it does and can be perceived in no other way. You might be the kindest person on earth, but if you were never heard to utter a kind word or seen to do a kind deed, how is anyone to know? The isolation of the self from its actions reduces personality to a thing having no consequences, a blank that is the stuff of madness—and riots. I can think of no more certain guarantee of disaster than idleness at any stage, and for the old it's murder. Or suicide. In any case, extinction.

I could wipe out ninety percent of old people's woes at a stroke by finding them suitable work. Finding, I said, not handing out. That's just more of what we've already got too much of. Lump thinking. Kneading people to fit the same size pans and baking them according to recipe. Work for old people has nothing to do with economic indicators and presidential commissions and policy makers snorkeling in a think tank. Oh, look here: any nation has to have policies, but they're meant to be a general hint, not an idol everyone's got to fall down and worship whenever the trumpet blows. Policy was originally a gambling term. We still speak of insurance policies, meaning what the odds are, nothing more. Being old isn't policy, it's a severely private enterprise, as I keep saying because *life* is that, and old people are alive, which is the first thing planning boards ought to notice and don't because they don't believe it.

Old people have brain and hands the same as anyone else, and these don't wither away unless they're persuaded into it. You can produce entropy and regression in an infant or an adult in his prime if you have a mind to. Age is not the controlling factor. The controlling factor is nothing to do. A working mind throws off threats and notions and outside opinions as spontaneously as a spinning wheel casts off a stone tossed at it. Work is health; work, not just a job. Yes, there is a difference, but later. Just now I want to tell you a story.

A friend of mine is one of those legendary western women clad in chinos and managing a ranch the size of Lichtenstein, and somehow looking more elegant than any big-city counterpart. Twenty-odd years ago she took her aging father off his subsistence farm in Iowa and brought him to live on the ranch. She hadn't seen him since she ran away from home at ten, and she didn't like him much then. But he was old and broke and had nobody else. Displacing him from all he'd ever known and fitting him into a guest room with a private bath, not to mention the family's affections and social life, was a sticky business.

She was wise enough to assign him a share of the chores, explaining that it was a working ranch and everyone on it pulled his weight. One of his jobs was to water the young trees that had recently been planted along the drive to the main gate. This entailed figuring out how to get the water down there, whether by coupling hoses to a storage tank or trucking it down in cans or some other means. One day my friend looked out the window and saw her youngest son, home from college on vacation, directing the hose while his grandfather stood in the road.

She went into the courtyard and rang the steel triangle that would bring all the compound hands on the double, except her father to whom it did not apply. She told the men they were there to hear what she would say to her son as it was intended for them all. Then she said no one was ever to take over the old man's tasks. "I know you mean to be kind," she said, "but it only shames him to do his work. It's not just a matter of keeping him busy; it's his whole right to be here. If you think I'm overworking him, come and tell me, but not him. I won't have him made worthless."

That just about says it all, and if I were half as smart as I like to think, I'd leave it there. But I won't. I'm a writer—what do you expect? I would God every old person had somebody that savvy and that courteous to redeem him. My friend never did come to love her father—she scarcely knew him—but she gave him something a thousand times more dear in both senses of the word, more to be cherished and more costly. She gave him self-respect, the right to be counted among men. He really did pull his weight. He knew it and so did everybody else. Maybe at its best that is love, but it's not sentimentality, and sentimental love could never achieve it. That kind of humane perception costs the utmost one can pay: energy, imagination, the setting aside of one's own preference, ease, justification.

Work keeps one geared into the whole crazy beautiful unfinished world where something always needs to be done and another pair of hands is always welcome. Or another good mind brought to bear. One is not required to sweat or to stick at it eight hours a day. After a certain number of years, the acceptance of a different pace, a shift in emphasis, is the mark of a supple understanding. But the boundaries are about where one chooses to put them. I knew an old man confined to a wheelchair who taught old-fashioned shoe repair, real cobbling, to paraplegic veterans. He had to do it all vocally—he could not use his hands so much as to feed himself—but he made a part-living teaching, and he showed those who still had hands a way to make a whole living.

Kindly do not speak to me of hobbies. I loathe the word. Comes from the same origin as *hobble*, and to my mind that's dead on target. Cutting out paper dolls is distraction for cranky tots or therapy for the sick but insulting to adults. Real work and real education, that's the open secret of satisfaction from birth to death. Work means consenting not to be the sheltered one; looking to oneself to provide purpose and variety; sharing the common hardships and thus the triumphs, if any, and if the whole project slides into the abyss, perishing with everybody else. Why not? You're going to perish anyway, far better to do it in self-respect. The Greeks had the right idea: death is nothing special, it is how one dies that measures the soul, and me, I'd rather die of hard work than some of the ways and places I can think of dying these days. At the very least one can be caught doing those things that properly belong to *homo sapiens*—learning, aware, not idle, not spiritually mendicant, even, God willing, laughing a little. The rule is, then, if you would not be shoved aside on a shelf, work at something.

I have a neighbor who at eighty-two serves three afternoons a week—a total of six hours—in a nursing home. She counts linen, carries trays, reads aloud, acts as ombudsman. We tease her gently about waiting on "old folks" who are often ten years her junior, but she says she doesn't tell them, and anyway it shapes her week. If one is not of use, she asks, why cumber the world? *Shape* is the operative word. Work, like education, is a way of ordering life, and life left to itself is unruly. It has to be; nature made it so in order to insure a continuity on sheer surplus if nothing else. It is the one lone insignificant mortal who gives life form, tang, grace, by shaping the material at hand as a sculptor shapes clay or granite. A single human life is a work, in the best artistic sense, though often people don't know it and thus make a botch of it. Who was it—Hugh Kenner at Johns Hopkins, I think—who said our biggest need is to get over not knowing what we're doing?

Oh well, I've heard that all my life—that the work ethic is just so much outdated piety, but *that's* only so much muddle-headed unreason. Those old puritans like the prophets before them had quaint ways of expressing themselves, but they knew a lot. They had guts enough to look within themselves for the faults that plague mankind, that's why. I don't see any shining evidence that current theories of no-ethic have outsmarted them.

They said we were born to work. It only means we're born ingenious; what's so grim about that? Me, I like being told I'm inventive, resourceful, adroit, quick, flexible, adaptable—all words my dictionary uses to define ingenious. Without work we are like Chinese shadow puppets made of muleskin—flat. When they turn their heads, the neck is seen edge-on, with no dimension. It's charming entertainment, but there's more to us than being amusing and amused. Somebody has to stand beneath the stage and work the rods that give the puppets animation. I'd rather be a worker than a semblance, wouldn't you?

The people I'm indebted to are not my moral instructors with whom I often disagreed, but the schoolteachers, employers, and editors who all my years including this one demanded work of me. They gave me a place to stand and skills to make of it whatever I would. That's like giving someone the

Comstock lode; it's still got to be worked but it's unbounded riches to anyone who will accept the terms.

I once interviewed a man who had retired a few years before as president of a major United States corporation. He and a partner, now dead, had more or less built the company from a rented corner in somebody's garage to a multimillion-dollar operation, so it was perhaps more his baby than some other firms are to their executive officers. Retiring was like being lynched for a crime he hadn't committed.

The company eased the break by giving him a posh office with elegant furnishings and a spectacular view but, as he said to me, empty all the same. At first his former associates dropped in for a mid-morning chat or asked him along to lunch. But more and more they talked of projects he wasn't privy to, and he fell silent. They began to bypass his door. No mail came; the phone did not ring. One day he tapped out a letter of thanks on a borrowed typewriter and left—permanently, as he should have done in the first place.

He salvaged one thing: the episode made him think. He was still the man who had virtually invented the company, dammit, and that meant his past career had not stemmed from the company so much as the other way around. He rented a one-room office in a dowdy building and set up shop as a consultant to independent and beginning enterprises. He didn't need money, so he worked for nothing until he found it made people uneasy—quite rightly—so he began taking fees. He turned the money over in no-strings grants to private liberal arts colleges that held no lure for government and foundation funds. He began to visit them and got interested in their problems, both financial and academic. They talked, he listened, and if he could think of a possible solution, he presented it. This time he was adamant about no payment. He would only hand it back to them, and why go to the expense of all that bookkeeping?

In short, he concocted a new kind of work in which the catastrophe of retirement was a positive asset: he had no personal axe to grind. He worked for achievement, not for success. There's the distinction between a job and work, by the way. A job is what one does to make a living; work you do because it *is* living. I'm being capricious with words, but not totally. A job is no shabby thing, even when it's the wrong one at the wrong time. It's an improvement on idleness. Any job swirls the mental and emotional molecules into perceiving the possibilities of doing something better. Ernest Hocking says in a book about human nature that it is often necessary to venture a wrong way in order to find a right one. Unused faculties can keep one frozen forever in inaction and indifference. The creature side of us likes comforts, but they numb the spirit. The vital side of us wants to employ its powers.

I'm not saying success can just be dismissed. Obviously that man had to get some results to show for his new efforts. To hold oneself aloof from all visible evidence and claim to be some superior kind of success is cloud-cuckooland. But I am using success in all its purple and ermine—big money, notoriety, applause, deference, titles, thick carpets, clout. What one suddenly comprehends in a working old age is the utter transparency between success and failure. They are not antagonists but the obverse and reverse of the same coin. Both involve going out on a limb, and what follows after attaining either one is exactly the same thing: going out on the next limb. Success is apt to be more fatal because one so fanatically deludes himself that the limb will extend forever. Neither success nor failure is the final word.

The so-called fear of success and the stress of being at the top arise from a question that comes at two A.M.: what if I can't keep it up? What about tomorrow, the next show, the next ballgame, the next election or advertising campaign or capital decision, the next operation, the next book? Ninety percent of success is measured by what other people think—or even crazier, what we think they'll think. Epictetus said if you base your self-esteem on being Caesar's friend and tomorrow Caesar is overthrown, then who are you? Oh, bet on it; Caesar is as vulnerable as you are. More.

To succeed simply means to follow in sequence. One succeeds to a throne, a rank, a position, only by replacing whoever held it before you, and it follows as the night the day that you will in turn be succeeded. Only age or retirement or experience—which are all more or less the same thing—sets one beyond all that and it no longer holds any terror. One outlives ambition and work takes on the clarity of being its own reward.

Perhaps the most successful man I ever encountered was a French Dominican monk named Raymond Bruckberger. During the Nazi occupation of France in World War II he obtained a dispensation from his order and joined the Maqui, the underground resistance fighters. He didn't carry a gun, he served as chaplain, but the Germans captured him twice and he escaped twice. He wasn't exactly young at the time, he was over fifty. He stood on the steps of Notre Dame cathedral and welcomed Charles de Gaulle back to Paris in 1944. After it was over, he returned to the monastery where among other things he wrote deep-searching books, and it was in that connection that I met him twenty years later. He was a big man with white hair and the countryman's relish of simple good food, the scholar's at-homeness in ancient languages. He wore that aura of total self-possession that clothes only those who have dared the full range of failure for a principle. I have never quite understood the need for role models, but if I were to have one, it would be that cowled monk.

Work is management, running things instead of being run, the use and direction of energies and resources, making choices. If one turns all that over to others—to family, lawyers, doctors, an abstraction called the government which is only a bunch of people not necessarily wiser than you are—one cannot then rightly complain of how they do it. I mistrust people who do things for other people's good. However well-intentioned they start out, they soon fall into the habit of acting from their own judgment, and ignoring the person in their charge. That's not because they're sly; it's built into the situation, and it's full of danger on both sides.

Human beings are born to inner autonomy that ought never to be surrendered to others except temporarily and on very good grounds. Oh, to the pilot of an airliner, the captain of a ship, a judge, a fireman in special circumstances—in fact, to a variety of specialists in certain circumstances. Sometimes in sickness, but not always. There is a story about George Bernard Shaw that when he was dying at ninety-four he forbade his doctors to give him any drugs. He said, "I'm not going to stay alive for your vanity!" It may not be true, but it's in character, and the point is highly important. Ownership of one's mind and body is the most basic of human rights, in a real measure undergirding all the others.

People in general are brainwashed into accepting resignation from self-responsibility as a well-deserved benefit of attaining a specified age, and it's sheer propaganda. Well, by unions, politicians, the medical clique, actuarians, admen, one's relatives for mercy's sake, anyone with something to gain in power, prestige, money. The best insurance against falling victim is to go on working, because work requires precision, decision, effectiveness in the hard-edged marketplace and therefore effectiveness as a person. Sure you'll make mistakes; when didn't you ever? Mistakes are one of the best roads I know to competence, awareness, ease in one's own skin.

I met a woman in retail management who had the unenviable task of firing an old man who plainly wasn't interested in the job any more. She stalled around until she figured out a way that seemed kinder than some others. She sat him down and began, "Mr. Smith, we in management are wondering if you haven't outgrown this job," and he quickly cut in.

"I know that but I didn't think you did. Two months ago I was offered a better job, and I couldn't think how to tell you without insulting the company. How soon do you think I could leave?"

The notion that work is a burden everyone seeks to escape is pure moonshine. Mandatory retirement began as a political ploy during the great depression, one means of coping with too many workers for too few jobs. The cutoff age of sixty-five was pulled out of a hat; there is nothing logical, let alone holy, about it. Congress still fiddles with it. In prosperity they lowered it to an optional sixty-two to show what good guys they were, spreading out the largess; and in times of inflation and towering federal debt, they debate about moving retirement up to sixty-seven or more to ease the drain on social security funds and the load on younger taxpayers. And they are trapped in their own sales pitch: how to do it without making themselves into bad guys, and who has the most votes in the medium run, the young or the old? You will forgive me if I find that funny. One thing Congress has never even flirted with is mandatory retirement for Congress. That's unthinkable.

The despair, loneliness, ill health, and confusion inflicted by compulsory idleness is no less than that imposed by compulsory labor, and there is a sense in which the former is worse: the pervasive myth that retirement is a great boon and one ought to be enjoying his misery.

In the 1950s I began to serve on the council of the Authors Guild, in effect its managing board. A continuing issue, I soon learned, was possible payment to authors for the use of their works by libraries. A certain novel topped the sales charts just then, and one council member who knew the author well said,

"If Joe could get one penny for every library loan, he could spend the rest of his life on the beach at Nassau and never write another line!" I was stunned. A fair return on borrowed books makes sense but was that the goal, to deprive a man of the work he loved and did best? I knew of course that it was a figure of speech, but how ingrained is the illusion of pleasant idleness that it could serve as such. It is commonly assumed that even schoolchildren would rather play than work, and in old age it is taken as a right, civil and humane.

Yes, it's unjust, and ignorant, but one cannot sit around waiting for justice to catch on—nor even walk the streets with placards demanding change, unless that happens to be one's calling, and all honor to those for whom it is so. I merely say there are other kinds of work, equally imperative. Politics is not life, no matter what the media gurus and politicos say—they find it so, it does not follow that everyone must agree. It took me twenty years to find out not everyone wanted to be a writer. There's a whole world out there crammed with all sorts of occupations and people to fill them—a good thing too, or what would writers write about? Besides, who then would be readers?

Forty years ago I published an article about what today would be called women's liberation. Made quite a few people mad, too, and maybe half a dozen very happy. One woman in her seventies tracked me down and took me out to lunch. She had a degree from one of the eastern women's colleges and had done battle in her day for women's academic rights. She'd been there and back, and she cautioned me to take note of a fact: that I was right for myself and those like me, but wrong for most women. She said most women would have loathed going to college in 1895, and they would be miserable, in the 1940s, leading my kind of career life.

"It will come," she said, "but not in my lifetime and not likely in yours. They also serve, who do *now* what the crusaders say can be done. One has just so much time and so much energy."

That woman did me great kindness. I saw that I could fight in a war—and it was already a long one—or I could do my work, but not both. Of course, war is some people's work, but that's different. Milovan Djilas—you know him? Yugoslavian freedom fighter and writer and twice vice-president—once said the critical point for revolutionaries is knowing how to stop. Having built a personal identity and a social fabric on fighting, they find it extremely hard to accept victory. When governing, not shooting, is what is needed, there have to be some who were victors in advance of the event.

Being old puts one in a position very like the feminist and the revolutionary. There is a lot of sweet talk about the enrichment old people bring to society, but nobody says what it is. Memoirs and oral history are about the best anyone can suggest, and I ask with the young, Who cares? Archives are valid, but the average person's recollections are boring.

Look: a child matures because it lives in a community where it is taught the mores of the group—everything from speech to family customs to the subtlest protocol. But the community evolves only by input from mature adults working singly outside the established code. That's what old citizens have to offer—the lucid dispassion that releases them from ambition, hurry sickness, ostentation. Now and only now is work done for itself and not for oneself.

I once asked Robert Frost when he was eighty-eight if he agreed, as many claim, that the most creative period is in youth, and he gave me a long blue stare. Then he said in his inductive way, "I wrote some things when I was twenty-five that I knew I'd never do better in my life. But I write poems now I couldn't even have conceived of at twenty-five—or fifty." That's how it is with any old person who listens to what's going on inside. Nonsense, it doesn't take genius, or if it does, it's the kind of genius available to all: paying attention, reflecting, caring for the small truths, not trying to be wonderful. An artist friend says if a man painted one masterpiece in his entire life, it was enough, worth all his other effort. He was old when he said it, of course. One doesn't know such things any sooner.

I've got a fat file on men and women who were high achievers in their seventies and eighties and nineties, many of them famous and historical figures, and twice as many not. I had planned to bowl you over with them, but all at once I see it won't do. And that's exhibit A of what I've been saying about work all along. If this project hadn't nudged me into thinking it through, I probably would have gone on supposing that file could prove my point. But it isn't really my purpose to show that exceptional people have done yeoman work in their late years. The point is that *anyone* can do it. I'd rather stir one lone insignificant mortal into believing that and running with it than prove that a thousand Toscaninis and Churchills and Santayanas did it. How sneaky are statistics. I was falling for them, too, wasn't I? The laws of probability and the laws in statute books can't save us. We as mature adults working singly have to save the laws, which is to say the community.

Oh, laws we must have. Let them be as fair as human wit can devise, but it's futile to imagine one can be legislated into good living at any age. To do one's work whether circumstances are for you or against you, and to remain flexible enough to drop the old work for the new, are about the only law one needs, and they come from within, not without.

A local resident who is a state senator came to my door campaigning for re-election. He gave me a list of laws he'd sponsored for the special benefit of older people and asked if I had any needs I wanted the state to act upon. I told him I felt it was my job not to become a public charge, and all I asked from the state was a reasonable protection and to be left alone to do my work. He blinked and said, "Well, that's a new one!"

I don't think it's new at all; I think it's very old. To work is one definition of being human. People no more want to be rid of it than they want to be dehumanized in other ways. As a smart Madison Avenue adman once said, human beings have a basic need to problem-solve, and to do it with a fair amount of consistency. I deplore his English, but his point is brilliant and hugely overlooked by social and political thinkers. My old friend Webster says a problem is a proposition set forth for solution. Where's the bane in that? A human being is a creature designed to find or invent solutions. The goal is not a programmed existence with all hazards removed. The goal is mastery, learning to cope with problems in creative ways—that is to say the goal is self-evolution. The adman in his hard-nosed wisdom saw that satisfaction comes only from the use of capacities to grow, do, become more—in short, from work. Power that is never employed is no power at all.

One reason the idle rich are a restless bunch is that they never have to call upon their inner resources to obtain all they can buy without thinking twice. Thus they conjure obstacles that will supply the appearance of achievement. Oh, such as going in for risky or forbidden objectives—running guns, seducing other men's wives, fiddling around with laundered money deals. Or making outrageous demands like ordering the Rolls in forget-me-not blue with their name engraved on the engine, whatever will delay immediate delivery and give the appearance of having been striven for.

The same specter of worthlessness haunts the idle old if society relegates them to that position—and if they let society do it. Well, no, you can't stop it, but you can forget society and find work to do. By all means, paid work. Nobody shells out real money for fake work, so payment is recognition on both sides that one is worth one's salt. It doesn't have to be big money and in rare cases not even cash. I know of a retired physicist and historian who writes learned articles and submits them free to any magazine that will take them. As his ideas are daring and his aim is to get them discussed, publication in itself is a form of remuneration. Besides, no editor yields up his columns just to be nice, so if he prints the material, there is again that tacit agreement that it's worth printing. But most of us can use money and should receive it in exchange for services rendered.

Ah, yes, volunteerism. It can be legitimate, even noble, but it wants watching. A young volunteer telephoned me to ask if I would be attending a cocktail party on behalf of a certain politician. I said no, and she replied, "But you will send your fifty dollars." *My* fifty dollars, you notice, and it wasn't a question. I asked why I should do that, and after thirty seconds of dead air, she gasped, "Well! Well, Mr. Jones is very good to his mother!" The trouble with volunteers is that they so often expect others to put up money for the projects they favor.

True service is a high order of human endeavor, but the motive for it is different from that which impels toward work. Service is, and will in most cases remain, unselfish and unheralded. Work summarizes one's whole posture in relation to living, to being involved in the productive world. It says "I can" to the universe. Work, or you lose the power to will, and that's what a self is. You can see it in a very young child who pushes away the hand that feeds it and grabs the spoon for itself. Work is the third dimension in which a human being substantiates himself. To say "I can" even when you can't, and then to make a try is to will, and in some small or great measure, you really do—at least in part. That's the whole ballgame—imposing one's elbow room on creation. Whatever halts or depletes that spirit is anti-human.

There always have been and will be special situations at the close of life, more or less short periods, when full dependency may be inescapable. But to foist it onto the entire populace twenty or thirty years before its time is reductionism. It assures people who could be useful to themselves and others that they are excess baggage.

Work is self-possession, helping one to accommodate change without losing the compass. That's not to say one always likes change, but a working man or woman at least avoids the double pitfall of clinging stubbornly to former patterns just because they are familiar or regarding all change as a conspiracy against oneself.

Work is dignity. It focuses worry on something worth worrying about instead of the body's miscellaneous aches and pains or the infighting of petty jealousies and imagined slights. Such trivial grievances are common enough in the workplace, but remember, I'm talking about work in old age, when egotism is no longer the big stake. It's there, but one keeps it on its shelf. Work promotes health, both mental and physical, because it calls for energy and in turn begets energy.

Work keeps one real. It is performance, not rehearsal, which is to say doing the thing itself. Any actor will tell you that one learns more from live performance than any amount of practice, necessary as that phase is. That's why plays have tryouts before live audiences. Performance is the final measure, where you pull it off or don't, and in the theater or in life one had better know.

To do is to be. Work may not be salvation but it comes very darned close—on this planet, about as close as we shall get.

VII

CURTAIN

Sorry I had to put you off last week, that deadline blew up out of nowhere. It surprises me these days; I no longer work at such a clip. On second thought, that's a polite social lie—that I'm sorry. I'm not. The whole episode illustrates so clearly all that I was saying before about the importance—the necessity—of work for the old. Work imposes unarguable demands and gives in return that critical sense of some things having to come first—shape, you see, the rescue of daily life from being flat. I just did a piece of work, on order, and now I'm feeling fat and sassy. It means we'll have a good session today. Shall we talk about dying?

Oh, glory, I can tell it's in your mind—you'd be hopeless if it weren't; that's where old age leads, after all. The great deadline no one can avoid—ha, that'll teach me to boast. You remind me of my old lawyer in New York days. He made me draw a will when I was thirty-two. I insisted it was silly, I had nothing to leave, and he retorted, "That's what you think. Anyway, it's a thing you ought to get used to."

He was right on both counts. I found a few modest items to dispose—a cameo, some rare books, a couple of copyrights. Made me feel quite propertied. Also made creepy things go up and down my spine. My heart thumped, my hand shook, and I thought, "This is my own death we're arranging!" I'm not really stupid, I had long known I would die someday, but until then my muscles didn't believe it. Now it was stark reality. I left the law office after signing the document feeling decidedly transient. I had to restrain myself from grabbing people on the street, making them notice me, and yelling, "Not yet! I'm still me and I'm still here!" Took me a week to recover my natural egotism.

I soon found out wills are made to be remade. Life goes on. Heirs die or get born; people get married or divorced; one acquires new property and sells off some of the old. After I'd done the thing over about three times, I understood the second half of the lawyer's remark, that I should get used to it. Arranging the results of my demise became routine, and far from unnerving me, the process made me feel safer, more real, in command. So ask your questions and don't suppose I shall be offended. And don't tiptoe. At my time of life death is a neighbor if not actually a friend. Maybe that too.

Well, you don't defy it exactly. That's apt to be bravado—and cheek. It's more nearly a mutual respect. Like two actors, a little jealous of one another, each with a role to play in a powerful drama and aware that neither can pull it off without the other. There is going to be a denouement in which the whole effectiveness depends upon each player's conviction that the other will give a strong performance. Does that make sense? Well, think, while I make some coffee.

I wouldn't go so far as to say come to terms, either. Not entirely. How can anybody do that when the terms aren't stated? What scares me a lot worse is the current medical scenario that bleaches death of all value, isolates it in a sterile room as full of gear as a TV studio, and destroys the human nature that alone redeems death by allowing its meaning. I once knew a county coroner in the west who said that all dead faces bear a certain nobility, even those of outcasts and failures, of tyrants, the embittered, the spiteful. I wonder if he could say that today?

The psychiatrist Howe, himself a medical man, said that doctors fear disease because they fear life, and I suspect they hate death because they do not know what life *is*. It forever eludes them. They know a thousand facts about its processes and can even duplicate a few, but those are not life itself. But it will take a major revolution to resolve that issue, and we shan't have time this afternoon.

What dying needs these days is a little common sense. Years ago I wrote an article about an old man—he was eighty-four—who was a bone specialist in a natural history museum. He was using a human skeleton to illustrate certain points and interrupted himself to say, "I call it 'he' because it is six feet tall, but the bones are very slender. It *could* have been a woman." I said that I thought scientists could always tell the sex. He gave me a funny look and reminded me gently that gender was a matter of the soft tissue, of no bearing whatever upon the bony structure inside. Afterwards I thought how true that was of almost all that human beings value about bodies—eyes, hair, sexual features, lean muscles, smooth skin—and how it all added up to trimming as far as skeletons went. It wasn't exactly comfortable, but most truth is not at first blush, and somehow it made me smile.

Crusty old Epictetus was a lot more ruthless. He was given to saying of even ordinary self-pride, "You are a little soul carrying around a corpse." That's marvelous. Maybe one has to be old to find it so, but I promise you the time will come when it will be not only funny but restorative. It sets me on my feet and spanks my bottom when I get solicitous of my flesh, my money, or my alleged cosmic standing.

Look here, I am not being flippant. This is solemn and unfathomable business, and one for which nobody gets to practice. My point exactly: an absolute one-time occurrence that is going to require all the skill one can muster deserves a little serious forethought. Not to say think about it all the while—that's a form of morbidity, which is only another way of ducking the issue. Not to say it will stay where you have thought it, either. But I do say, think it *through*. Then you can truly forget about it, the way you can forget about worldly goods after you've settled them in a will. Indeed it is to make again, and so are conclusions about death, but in the meantime, in both cases, one stops agonizing.

It's not all that difficult. Every day of our lives we process information. You could even say that's what a human being is: a system for economizing events, knowledge, impressions. What slowly becomes apparent as one nears the finish line is that death too is a piece of information to be processed within the limits of one's personality. A persuasion of immortality would certainly help, but even if one is locked into linear time, the call to face the blank end of it without flinching is a call to some measure of greatness.

I am one who leans toward immortality but that is not a conviction one can just hand over to anyone else. Come back next year if you want a full dissertation on life after death. I'll only say now that I try not to be soppy about it, nor do I hold such views from fear. It's no use supposing immortality will obviate the need for courage; I expect it's a lot of hard work like any other stage of life. Of course I can't prove it, not the way you mean prove. And if I could, it would kill it, which is at least hilarious. Proof of immortality in worldly terms would make it cease to be immortal, and just one more scientific thesis, defined and contained in careful space-time parameters. Like most things religious, people don't really want the implications of immortality. They want it both ways at once: out of this world and confirmed by this world. Remember that I said not everything needs to be said? Well, not everything can be said either. That's one of the notions we have to give up, and it's mostly the old who are prepared to do it.

There are ways of knowing, Horatio, that are unimaginable to the clipboard thinkers, and so are despised. As one physicist put it to me with a grin, "If there are such realities as you infer, we don't want to know about them. We would have to rethink our whole approach, and that we do not wish to do." It takes audacity to face death and what the Spanish call *el más allá*—means the *beyond* but it translates literally into "the more there," which is a whole philosophy in three words. Anyway, audacity is the requisite commodity and it's one of the boons of old people. That's why so much of what they say sounds outrageous.

This is another thing we old ones share with very young children, this intimacy with realms outside the accepted measurements. In children it is implicit, and their problem is to disengage from it enough to make headway in the world, while for those at the far rim the difficulty is letting go of existential techniques learned too well. At both extremes of the lifespan, though, the knowledge is present just below the surface, much as awareness of the ocean is present for people living just back of the coastline. It's comprised of a thousand signs imperceptible to inland dwellers: the wideness and translucence of the sky; the softening of salt-laden air, tasted on the lips before the nose can smell it; the roadside grasses and the way they yield to the prevailing winds; the change in pressure on one's skin; the rote of the surf felt in the blood while still too distant to be heard; the low-lying hills and the rough stubby trees crouching in the gullies; the stirring of ancestral memories not quite remembered.

When my mother was seventy-five, a Swiss company built an aerial tramway near her mountain home, rising 10,000 feet from the valley floor. A funicular, like a ski lift only bigger. None of the people she knew would go near it, so when I came to visit, she asked if I would ride it with her. It was no more dangerous than an elevator and far less so than a car or plane, but it was eerie. It was almost silent, and it threw off one's ordinary sense perceptions. We looked down upon treetops and huge boulders, but close-to so that the usual relation to the earth was upside down. It reminded me of being in a funny-house where walls and floors are built askew and one leans over on a slant, desperately trying to get things straightened up normally.

At the top was a chalet where visitors could buy lunch and take it outdoors on a wide deck cantilevered over empty air. The car going up held some sixty people, and we had got chatty with a Dutch engineer hung with expensive cameras. As we climbed the broad shallow steps to the restaurant, puffing a little in the thin air, the Dutchman glanced at my mother and said quietly to me, "The heart is good?" I gestured to my head and said, "The heart is good up here."

He smiled. "Of course, I should have known. I travel all over the world and everywhere it is the same. The old are braver than the young."

"Why?" I asked. "Because their time is short and they have less to risk?"

"Oh, no." He shook his head. "Because they are farther up the mountain and can already see there is no risk."

Now I am beginning to understand what he meant. In youth death seems like an affront or a dirty trick.

In age it is a wiping clean of the slate, a cancellation of old debts in both directions. I myself have actually seen only three people die, all old people, and each spoke of a singular gentleness toward others, absolving them of all grievances. Most astonishing to me was their feeling in a *position* to absolve them, as though they had attained a level above routine human abrasion and attrition. Samuel Johnson was being foxy when he said the knowledge of imminent death wonderfully concentrates the mind, but like all true wit it was piercingly accurate.

As the final curtain begins to lower, death takes on possibilities, weird as that may sound. I find myself at times immensely curious, and curiosity can get you through a lot. All societies have been confounded by death—it simply does not fit man's self-concept—but it is said no civilization has held it in such terror as our own. If that is so, it's partly because we are mesmerized by progress. Death thumbs its nose at our immense improvements, and, like my physicist friend, that upsets us. We are so blazing sure we have licked many evils, how dare death endure? Don't look back. *¡Adelante!*

Right there lies the trouble. The vital movement in life is not progress, straight-line advance—toward what? I always want to ask. Where can we go on a round earth, in an orbiting solar system, a spiraling galaxy? The primary motion is reciprocity, rhythm, what scientists sometimes call resonance. All creation is based on it: the blinking of the eye, the cadence of the heartbeat, the indrawing and expelling of breath; the ebb and flow of tides, planting and harvest, the coming and going of the seasons—why not of the human person? Birth and death are a unit. To welcome one and deplore the other as if they were antagonistic *makes* them antagonistic, and makes us homeless in the universe.

Old age is a profound instruction in living without vanity. That's not entirely easy—one has had so long to practice all the little conceits—but the alternative is harder: living out the last years crabbed and angry and afraid. And fiercely denying the lot, as if one could make it not so. The two biggest blunders in life are refusal to commit oneself and refusing to let go when the time comes—of jobs, of children, of position, of habits, and of course of life itself. Age is a kind of grace period in which to get used to the idea. And what a jolt. As the old props crumble, one discovers—how unwillingly and how late—that one can stand without props, and walk and run and ski and dance. And *that* begins to be not against one's will at all.

Yes, I think the old do tend to get religion, but not from fear—from an increased openness to what religion has been saying all along. The sheer geographical proximity of death shows survival to be a dream, and one casts around for other values. To my mind, religion is taught much too soon, a bad mistake for both parties, the learner and religion. It is the language that misfires, but it's not language alone; it's even more our built-in deafness, what the Bible calls ears dull of hearing. It takes time to get cured of that.

Most people, I think, seek some kind of unity. Our whole lifetime we are quite literally pulling ourselves together, collecting the ten thousand fragments as the Greek poet said. There's nothing wrong with that;

it serves, it teaches, it builds, and if one has managed a little self-knowledge here and there, at the outer edges he gets a chance to scatter himself again and maybe recollect in another dimension. One turns a corner and comes suddenly face to face with the pure essence with which it all began, the reality outside the sensory world. Not opposed to it, oh no—a very logical outcome of having lived it. One comes around again and yet does not go back. It is the eternal helix, the revolving of time and space with oneself caught up in it, for we are surely not apart from the universal process. Resonance, reciprocity, white water folding, tumbling, turning back upon itself yet flowing ever on.

You won't catch old people saying much about it. It embarrasses others for one thing—you're a little edgy right now—and then, too, the need to speak abates. It becomes more and more difficult to explain oneself but less and less necessary. Only stubborn types like me persist, and we need our heads examined.

It's not possible, but when was impossibility an excuse for failure to try? How shall I say this? There are moments in the life of the old—for me, walking at the edge of the sea, listening to the Berlioz *Requiem*, standing quiet on a winter evening as the house draws in around me—moments when I perceive myself so completely to be that one lone insignificant mortal that it snatches the breath from me. I cannot tell you how exalting that is. Oh, no, it doesn't erase me, it unifies me, makes me so crystal clear that I am transparent—and *alive*. It's not unlike the shafts of sunlight piercing the redwood forests of my childhood when I stood transfixed in two realms at once. When it happens in full age, one knows what it is he feels and sees and is ready to bear the responsibility and the joy.

It doesn't last, not yet. One moves into that other realm only by stages. But old people have a foot in each of two worlds, so that for them expectancy toward death is a perfectly natural cast of mind. It is nature's way of preparing us to wind up our contract with this phase, an awareness of a bargain fulfilled that eliminates terror and holds out promise. Only those lagging behind fancy that it must be otherwise.

Leave it now. We have said all we can for the present on this great mystery.

VIII

A TIME FOR SORTING

You know anything about Oriental calligraphy? Here, I've drawn you a Chinese character—not very well. It doesn't look right unless it's done with a brush, and I've never mastered one. But it's a beautiful idea. Those two little tree things are leafy branches, and the gizmo just below is a hand; the combination means broom. That open box is a heart and the three globs going through it are pulse beats. Literally translated it comes out "clean-swept heart," and what it means is "wisdom." Isn't that nice?

Most cultures credit old people—if they credit them with anything at all—with wisdom. It doesn't arrive automatically with years, and yet it does rather if one clears out enough clutter. And that's what old age is, in a sense: a time for sweeping. Or what the Scots call sorting. If two workers are not getting along, the manager will say, "I've got to go and sort those chaps." Or a crofter says of a spring clogged with winter debris that it needs sorting. It's the original usage of the word, meaning to separate out, to select, to distinguish one matter from others. One does a lot of that after sixty, not trashing the entire past but neatening it up, brushing the litter from a lifetime, and seeing what's left of value. The skimpiness of what's left is unsettling but more real than those other selves one has paraded around in—the me in me one has deeply felt must be there somewhere. In age it is reality one yearns for, not saving face.

If my Dutchman was right, that there is more daring in old people than the young, it is largely because they wield a thicker broom. Society in general attaches little importance to the old except in the philosophical abstract—"wisdom" has a pleasing sound, but we will kindly keep it to ourselves. It's understandable: society would collapse under the scrutiny of wisdom, and its aversion is not entirely a bad thing. Being brushed off works a backhanded freedom for the old. One is released not only to think in utter honesty but to take over control of the traffic in one's own head—and that *is* wisdom.

It's rather shocking how many obstacles are not inherent in passing time but are imposed from without by those who fear age and clutch fiercely their own unstable youth. Take the word "still." How often do you hear, "She is still very attractive" or "He still plays tennis"? She's still teaching piano; he still practices law. People say of me that I'm still writing, keeping my own house, going to baseball games, swimming in the ocean. Not long ago I heard a man say to a woman of forty-five, "You're still a beauty, you know that?" High praise in his view, but I would have clobbered him. What a miserly word is still. All the worse for ignorance of its big muddy boots. It tramps over the feelings, as if what was naturally one's own when one was younger is now a miracle, even almost freakish. Admirably so, perhaps, but none the less leaning heavily on one—in the police sense—to settle down and behave in the proper decrepit style.

Memory loss is another cliché that rankles with the nonaged, as if it somehow threatened or cast aspersions on themselves. Maybe it does; maybe it suggests that the recall of which they boast is tedious? The woman with whom I played the game of learning five new words a week deliberately cultivated *not* remembering. She said all that excess baggage weighed her down and she preferred to travel light. It is anyway a novel approach, and at least she wasn't cowed by memory, pro or con. And I must say for her method that even in her nineties, I never knew her to flub a line or grope for a piece of information.

Memory loss is not the franchise of age. A small child hopping from one foot to the other for a chance to speak finally gets his turn and promptly goes blank. Adults may smile or dismiss the child impatiently, but nobody charges him with failing faculties. Yet when it happens to an old person, heads shake sadly, talk surges in like a wave to cover the social gaffe, or open apologies are offered for poor dim mother.

There is a story I like about Queen Mary—the old queen, grandmother to Elizabeth II—whose memory began to play tricks. But nobody condescends to a queen or talks rudely over her head, and she remained unruffled. One day in conversation with a visitor she suffered several lapses, and, well aware of the fact, she announced regally, "They tell me I have lost my memory, but I *mean* to get it back!"

The rest of us would do well to take a leaf from the queen's book. We all have more royalty than we faintly suspect or dream of using. It's only authority after all, power to command, and what most needs commanding in any life is oneself. Nobody wholly escapes aging—I'm not sure we want to; it would be kind of tasteless—but it is possible in almost any circumstances and, I believe, imperative to meet age bravely, wittily, and with some degree of dominance. Self-styled helpers who belittle that capacity are like Job's alleged friends in the Bible, eager to help him into assorted sins that would account for his difficulties. But Job wasn't having any, thank you all the same. He growled at them, "Miserable comforters are ye all!" You cannot truly help anyone by taking away his basic humanity, his initiative, courage, independence.

Agism in so far as I have encountered it—I take it to mean the appraisal of age as an offense—has all been of that do-good variety. It means well, God help us. Nobody has yet slammed a door in my face or spat on me, but I am besieged to accept free passes on city and state transit, up-front seats at movies and ballgames, automatic pension increases when the cost of living says so, never mind what I say; discounts at stores on stated days, prepaid drugs and hospitalization, absentee ballots for voting at home—all on the grounds of entitlement, for which I am not required to do one blamed thing except breathe the set number of years. Is it immoral to suppose that grown human beings should contribute something toward their own existence?

Ah, I've heard that argument before. You're saying, Take the bus pass and you'll have it in case. That's the camel's nose in the tent. Inevitably an "in case" arises. One is low on pocket money for the fare, or the car has a flat tire, and instead of using one's brain to deal with the situation, a nasty thought occurs: a free ride just once won't corrupt me. You've had it; you've bought the sales pitch. Entitlement by now is an industry, and, like any other, it pushes its product. The steady drumbeat is insidious: Perhaps I do deserve to rest; maybe I'm not such a good manager as I like to think; possibly I'm a poor sort of citizen for not following the crowd—after all, that's democracy, isn't it? If food prices soar, who am I to adjust by planning cheaper meals? When gasoline goes up, what gives me authority to consolidate my trips into town or even walk, heaven forbid? If I can get into the movies cheap, am I not being snobbish to pay the regular admission? In short, who do I think I am to function like a rational adult in my dotage?

When I became eligible for social security, I made the government a proposition. I said: Give me a modest lump—less than they would pay me if I survived just five years—and let me manage it and I will never ask for another penny. It gave them fits, of course. There was no law to cover such an arrangement; if they did it for me, they would have to do it for others; it would give the computers hiccups. And above all, what gave me to think I knew how to manage my affairs better than the government? I might have said, but did not, that the government wasn't doing too brilliantly just then since the system was on one of its periodic verges of bankruptcy. I could have pointed out that by investing it, I should at least be contributing to the economy instead of rolling it back to the government as taxes, which is mainly what happens now. But they gave me a lot of talk about entitlement, and I had expected nothing else. I just wanted to find out what they'd do.

If—not when but if—I am no longer able to cope, I shall accept aid from a charitable society with, I hope, good grace, but until then I will thank the powers that be not to meddle. Aid, I said, not subsidy, which derives from a French verb meaning to sit down. If I could make a motto for all governments, it would be *Let well enough alone*. Indiscriminate subsidy is reductionism, I care not what labels are pasted over it. Compassion also has a pleasing sound, but does no one realize that giving is a subtle form of domination? He who picks up the tab calls the shots, as I told that doctor, and quite rightly. That's why old people hang onto the shreds of autonomy; it's not just blind-fool stubbornness. It's also why teenagers are eager to earn their own money.

Entitlement is a cover word for second-class citizenship. I'll take accountability any day. It might do me in before my time, but I hadn't planned to live forever, and I'd rather be dead dead than living dead, which I see a fair amount of.

Am I going on too long? Old people get their knuckles rapped for garrulity and no doubt we merit it, but if we do, so does nearly everybody else. It's not senile, it's human. I know a dozen people whose conversation is so redundant I could write the script, but because they are in their thirties and forties they are called neurotic or depressed or high-spirited or even artistic, God help us—but not old. When young people howl about their elders' constant prattle, I want to ask how they endure the same television commercials six, eight, a dozen times a day, week in and week out, month after month for over a year? Even when the advertisement is entertaining, which is seldom, the battology becomes an insult to the mind, in the strict medical sense, yet the young seem impervious. I venture to guess it is because they equate TV with their own time—sleek, mod, savvy, part of the action. It isn't grandma's talkiness that gravels them, it's her age.

People speak pretty much as they are spoken to. Screech at them and they'll screech back. Spout inanities and you will get inane feedback. That too is not old behavior, it's people behavior. Babies, teenagers, the lot, even animals in their mute fashion. A friend and I, both ranking as old, went to visit an even more ancient woman in a nursing home, one of whose maladies was blathering on disconnectedly about nothing sensible. We talked with her and with one another as we would have done in any small social group—about people she knew, who the next mayor might be, the recipe for her famous butterscotch brownies, the new shopping center—and she soon joined in so normally that the nurses stood by in disbelief. Poor woman, I don't think anybody had talked sense to her for a long time.

Hoosh, I grant you it would be hard going twenty-four hours a day, but I bet I could do it if it were my job—and it is my job *for me*. How one talks to oneself creates the world one lives in more than any other single factor, and with a little effort the internal dialogue is subject to one's control.

But the point here is that old people don't live in a vacuum. They live like all human beings in a context, and whatever ails them at least halfway ails the context. If we really want to enrich life for pensioners, we have to start with the climate into which they are plunged. By that I mean the rock-hard theories, assumptions, procedures, and expectations of a society that knows everything about abstract age and nothing about living breathing men and women.

If old people are forgetful, I'll tell you what young ones are—ignorant. They aren't to blame, it's congenital until it is outgrown. There's the rub: old-timers really do know a thing or two that others don't. The un-old postulate from total inexperience what their elders think, feel, want, and scull them into fitting the program in airy rapture over their own genius. They do not see that memory is not addled because of age. Memory too works in a context, and by sixty or seventy the contexts are so varied and crowded it's a blooming wonder the human creature retains all it does. We are a mobile nation. I myself have lived in three states and a dozen cities, and put down roots in all of them—and that's peanuts compared with most people's perambulations.

I saw my mailman in the supermarket, out of uniform, out of locale, out of his occupational groove, and I was halfway up the next aisle before I could place him. But not because my brain was going soft—

it happened forty years ago. I can get so saturated in the world issuing from my typewriter that I pass acquaintances on the street unseeing, and if they speak I am jerked up sharply and have to grope to think who they are and what relation they have to me. But neither is that *ipso facto* dotage—indeed it was worse when I was young because of my naive conviction that everybody thought writing as important as I did. Lately I've got more professional.

We must be careful not to leap to other people's conclusions, no matter how rational, *when they don't compute with one's own lived life*. Obviously, specialists sometimes know more than we do, but being wrong and genuine gets one further than being right and a fake. It is an old person's plain business to be a little truculent, to be aware of other sides to things, to do away with excuses and indulgences. Human life is untamable. By seventy one knows that the minute you get it sorted, life will slap you down and go off on a tangent of its own, and human glory is that we pick ourselves up and figure it out again. The old can give themselves at least honorable mention for having toughed it out thus far.

Bah, I don't believe in regret. We do the things we do when they have meaning for us, or when we think they have, and it comes to the same thing. To refuse to act along that line warps the soul far worse than choosing the wrong action. To err is not stupidity, it is how one learns to adapt, and adaptation to changing situations is a prime definition of intelligence. When as a child I heard adults say "If I had it to do over . . . ," I thought it shameful, though I didn't know why. I swore to live so smart I'd never have to use that sorry phrase. A pitiable resolution; being young is a kind of crime. But life sees to it. I've made my share of big fat mistakes and putting my foot wrong, but undo them? Not I. They made me. I still make mistakes, but now I know how to live with them.

Ah, that's different; there's plenty I would add but I figure I'll have a go at them next time around. Such as playing a musical instrument with others, in an orchestra or ensemble. I don't know enough about working in a group for a common goal. I shall never again go through a lifetime without fluency in at least one foreign language. I shall travel more in my youth. I'm not sure it matters in itself, but it's important to have done. Many things are like that, valuable mainly as background, but to attain that position they have to be done in their proper time. Oh, that's another thing: I want greatly to improve my timing. Music would help, and athletics. I shouldn't mind learning to ski—it is said to be the nearest thing to flight. I'd want to be good enough to do it in moonlight. All this is an argument for immortality, by the way. Nobody can possibly do in one lifetime all that is available to him, or learn all he wants to know, and since idea and ability attract one another, the prospect opens out endlessly. The more you do, the more you can conceive of doing. What's endless but eternity, h'm?

I think it very possible that life neither begins nor ends. We step out upon it at some point—whether voluntarily or not, I don't know; I'm working on it—and exit at a later time like players in a theater. The role is cast off, stage-time stops, but the actor offstage goes about his business in a life unconnected with the theater except in that he shall have performed well, whether bit part or lead.

In my playwriting course at which I kicked so much I learned that the difference between a live play and a dead one is that in the former the characters control the plot, while in the latter case the plot rules and characters are pushed about to suit its framework. Exactly the same can be said of a live and a dead old age. Life is not an illusion, but it is kind of half-real. In age it gets more transparent. It takes brains to be old. Never let outsiders squeeze you into their concept of what abstract age should be. It's a journey inward, and no one can know the country who hasn't lived inside your head. The two inescapable rules are that sooner or later one must grow all the way up and that the responsibility for that is one's own *alone*. There is no other way.

I coexist now with all my selves, and I am the only one who truly knows them. I've had what the British call a good innings. I have enjoyed immensely my encounter with the world, and now I don't quite believe in the world any more. The early years were not wrong or worthless, but they've served the purpose and are finished; they have no reality now. I look back on them as a kind of soap opera—there is a time for melodrama but I am elsewhere now.

Nor does the world quite believe in me; that's fair enough. Trying to compel an old romance is like trying to light a candle that has guttered out. The world no longer requires my services to sustain its self-belief, and so I am set free to require myself for my own aims. My assigned role now is to be old and the only question is whether I shall perform the part well. Certainly not if I refuse the casting director's choice.

I have learned to the limits of my present capacity that change is not catastrophe but growth, even drastic change. Life by definition is motion, there's no way around that. Form arises from asymmetry, or chaos if you like—Chaos was the first Greek god, remember—and dissolves back into it in order that fresh form shall emerge. There is a profound and satisfying dynamics in that, but one is not prepared to encompass such dynamics till one is old. Then the Christian teaching that one must lose one's life to find it comes dramatically alive. The Taoists say it this way, "To be and not to be are mutually conditioned." That is the secret secret.

You are determined I shall stick my neck out, aren't you? You want a list of dos and don'ts for how to be happy though antique. Very well, it's one of the few flatteries of age that people ask one such things. It happens that I made up a small list last night. Go ahead, laugh—I was hoping you'd twist my arm a little, and it's not easy to be pithy ad lib. Can you do it? I had to think long and chop ruthlessly, and that's good exercise, even if I had miscalculated your determination. Pay attention.

This first item is for society at large. Yes, just the one. As I've already said, one cannot do much about society; you might as well try to shift Mount Everest. But I make a plea for this one little thing which would alleviate a lot of misery, not to mention saving tax dollars: *Don't take the old for granted*. Whatever the un-old think they know about us, they don't and can't—until they've been there about ten years, and then what they'll know will be about themselves, not us.

People see an old person hesitating at a street corner, and what do they do? Grab his arm and hustle him across. It's offensive—a blind friend taught me that. Would they do it to a younger person? Even a lost child gets *asked* whether one can be of help. How dare they be so sure that the old person wants to cross the street? Maybe he's just amusedly watching the passing parade. Maybe he's waiting for a friend to pick him up in a limousine and take him to lunch. Maybe he's debating whether to go to the shop in the next block or if the one behind him will do just as well. The sin of taking for granted is its density which translates into self-righteousness. And in case my message is obscure, I'm talking about the curbstones and highways of life. A synecdoche—that's Greek for meaning it about the street corners but meaning something more as well.

All the other admonitions on my list are for individuals, including me. Sure I know what I'm saying, but one of the delights of being old is learning from one's own mind and keeping on learning at deeper and deeper levels.

Here we go: Don't fret; it's fidgety and life will go on being itself anyway. Don't pamper your body; *work* your body, that's what it was designed for and all it wants from you is work. Don't hoard money and don't throw it around; use it. Don't dabble in petty powers; find a real power and give it all you've got. Dance once a day. Yes, dance—what's weird about that? Dancing is the opposite of complaint. Oh, alone, like an otter in a waterfall or a cat stalking a windblown leaf, two animals that have located the fountain of youth. See beauty every day. Do the ordinary tasks well: cook or stitch or sweep, chop or dig, plant or repair. It keeps one real. Read one book a year that you know you will not understand.

Forget happiness and go for poise; the goal of living is poise, the swing between coordinates. Don't be a snob; nobody will believe you. And this may be the most important: Don't be a taker until you have exhausted every alternative you can think of, and if it comes to taking, give *something* in return, in goods or services, however small. The real world gives nothing for nothing. That's why I'm leery of entitlement—it decoys one into lotus-land as certainly as do drugs.

That's enough, probably too much. Making up aphorisms is great fun but it's the kind of thing that gives the old a bad name. We are supposed to keep our knuckles down bony tight. Didn't you ever play marbles? What's become of childhood? It means in this instance keep our bits of discovery below the gunwales so as not to rock the boat.

Look: I am not saying do it my way and live. My whole campaign is don't do it anybody's way but your own—and however your own may go, *take charge*. There is a difference between growing old and collapsing into it.

We are born asleep and it takes roughly forty years to wake up. That's where the saying comes from that life begins at forty. The French of course put it more frenchily: they say forty is the old age of youth and the youth of old age. The whole idea is very ancient. It is quite possibly the meaning of the Israelites' forty-year sojourn in the wilderness. One simply does not deal in reality—correction: does not accommodate other realities—until he has begun to disengage from the first one, and that just plain takes time. I know a hundred things I didn't know ten years ago—all right, a dozen things—and I also know that as fast as I get them assimilated a dozen new ones will rush in to grab my ears and blow my mind with concepts I cannot presently even imagine. That alone makes old age worth the candle.

Oh, for one thing, I love my work with a passion, but I no longer feel possessive of it. I have stopped needing an audience. Yes, but readers are different—they are the other half of what I do; it takes readers to complete it. But once a piece of work is in their hands, it belongs to them, not to me. One ultimately learns to work for the craft itself. This is true not only of the arts; it happens with any work aged in the wood. What it amounts to is manumission from trying to become something other or more than one already is. Age is the age of being, not becoming.

I have acquired some humility, which is intellectual patience. Thus I am better at friendship. I don't have to endorse everything another thinks or does in order to be his friend. One vein of congeniality is sufficient and the rest is none of my business. Nor do I, in reverse, expect wholesale approval from others. The best of friends will occasionally criticize and gossip; that's not only their human prerogative, it is part of what keeps them interesting. Unanimity soon palls. I even find myself liking a few people who do not at all like me, and it is oddly refreshing. It puts a dent in my ego that helps to keep my mutual attractions healthy. I measure friends for what they are themselves and not for what they make me.

In recent years I've learned to state my case without apology and without dogma. Most of the time. When I manage it for thirty days in a row, I go and make sacrifice to the gods. It is a taste of self-possession, and that's the whole ballgame.

I don't weep anymore in sorrow. About the only thing that makes me cry now is good work.

I am seldom angry, and when I am, it's not *at* somebody.

None of this sounds very enormous, I suppose, but it is to me. Age is yield time. I know myself as never before because my self is not exclusively identified with me. The boundary where I leave off and the not-I begins is not so sharp as it was, so that I can go outside and see myself, really see. Is that too woolly? Well, it'll come—or it won't. We all grow up at different rates, fast in some ways, slow in others, and what age reveals in each case depends upon what one has believed and acted upon before. Whatever it was, you may be sure age will turn it upside down and backwards.

I want to bring us back to kitchens and cooking fires. *Old* is a beautiful word, and I resent all the cute and clever and cowardly euphemisms that dodge around it. If you ever call me a senior citizen, I shall do something violent. In languages other than English, *old* is a title of honor, and we could make it so. To call someone *mon vieux* in French is a salute to experience. In Spanish it is the same with *el viejo*; in Italian, *il vecchio*; in German, *der Alte*. After World

War II, the Germans called Konrad Adenauer, their grand old chancellor who brought the nation back to respectability, *der Alte* in affection and in homage.

Go look up the word *old* in dictionaries. Its origins mean to grow up, to nourish, to produce—nothing dead in the water about that—and it also derives from *altus*, high, as in altitude and altar. When you and I first began to talk, I said that *focus* comes from the Latin for altar, too, do you recall? Well, then, we have come full circle. To age, to grow old and bear it well, is to center oneself in some complete and whole manner. Only by living do we release ourselves from living.

I shall miss you, too, but don't worry; the old are durable.